W9-ART-144

How To Draw

TANKS AND OTHER FIGHTING MACHINES

Illustrated by
Jael

Incorporated

Copyright © 2002 Kidsbooks, Inc.
230 Fifth Avenue
New York, NY 10001

Manufactured in Canada

Visit us at *www.kidsbooks.com*
Volume discounts available for group purchases.

INTRODUCTION

This book will show you how to draw lots of tanks and other military machines. Some will be more difficult to draw than others, but if you follow along, step by step, you will soon be able to draw tanks, planes, battleships, and more.

SUPPLIES

NUMBER-2 PENCILS   **FELT-TIP PEN**
SOFT ERASER   **COLORED PENCILS**
DRAWING PAD   **MARKERS OR CRAYONS**

Each drawing in this book begins with two or three free-form shapes. These establish the basic outline of the figure. Then various shapes—such as ovals, circles, and rectangles—are added to the figure to fill out the drawing.

HELPFUL HINTS

1. In the first two steps of each drawing, you will create a solid foundation of the figure (much like a builder who must first construct a foundation before building the rest of the house). Next comes the fun part: creating a smooth, clean outline of the machine, then adding all the finishing touches, such as details, shading, and color.

Note: Following the first two steps carefully will make the final steps easier.

2. Always keep your pencil lines light and soft. Doing this will make these guidelines easier to erase when you no longer need them.

3. Don't be afraid to erase. It usually takes a lot of sketching and erasing before you will be satisfied with the way your drawing looks. Each image has special characteristics that make it easier or, in some cases, harder to draw. However, it is easier to draw anything if you break it down into simple shapes.

4. Add details and all the finishing touches only *after* you have blended and refined all the shapes and your drawing is complete.

5. Remember: Practice makes perfect. Don't be discouraged if you don't get the hang of it right away. Just keep drawing and erasing until you do.

HOW TO START

1. Begin by drawing the basic overlapping shapes, such as the ones shown in step #1 below. This forms a general outline of the machine. Usually, it is easier to begin by drawing the largest shape first. The dotted lines show what can be erased as you go along.

2. Sketch the other shapes *over* the first ones. These are the basic guidelines that create the foundation of your drawing.

Remember to keep your lines lightly drawn, erasing any guidelines you no longer need as you go along.

3. Carefully combine and blend all the lines and shapes, so that the figure has a smooth look. Then begin adding the details that make this vehicle unique.

4. Complete the treads, engines, guns, rotors, and any other finishing touches. Color your finished drawing with your favorite colors or, for a more dramatic effect, outline it with a thick, black marker.

Use your imagination! Feel free to create details other than the ones shown here. You may even want to add backgrounds to enhance your drawings. When you have drawn some or all of the machines in this book and are comfortable with your drawing technique, start creating your own fearsome fighting machines.

Most of all, HAVE FUN!

Foreshortening
Some vehicles in this book are shown in dramatic ways that include foreshortening. *Foreshortening* is when parts of a figure are drawn shorter or smaller—as the eye sees them rather than as they really are. Artists use this technique to give figures a realistic, three-dimensional appearance. An example of foreshortening can be found later in this book, on the pages showing the M109A6 Paladin or the F-117 stealth fighter.

1.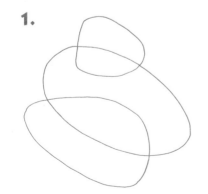

2.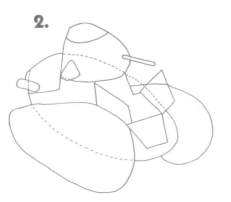

3.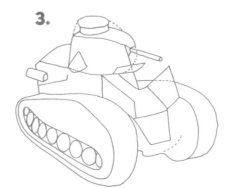

4.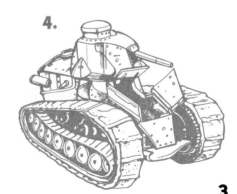

WORLD WAR II TANK

During WWII in Europe, tanks were an important part of the ground-war strategy for both sides.

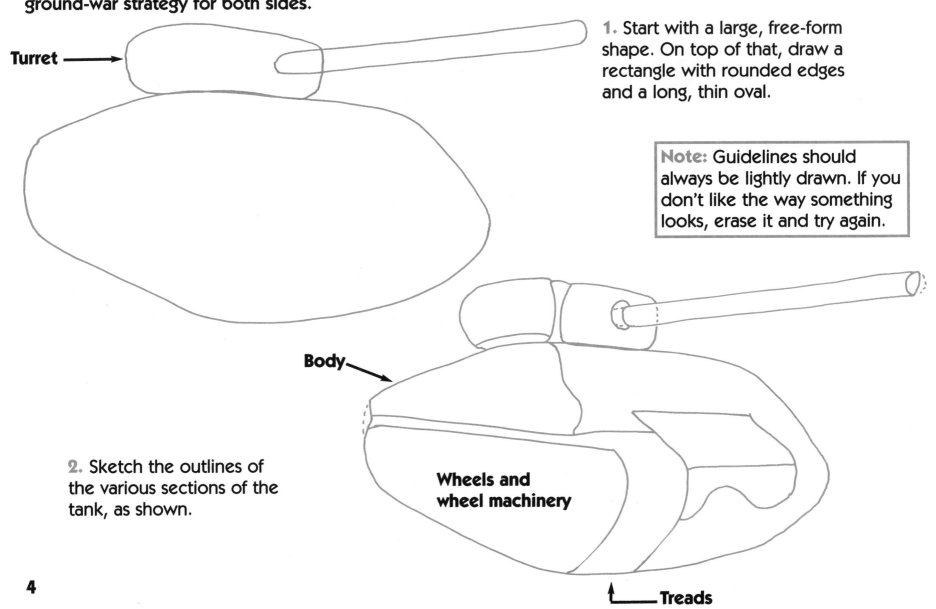

Turret

1. Start with a large, free-form shape. On top of that, draw a rectangle with rounded edges and a long, thin oval.

Note: Guidelines should always be lightly drawn. If you don't like the way something looks, erase it and try again.

Body

2. Sketch the outlines of the various sections of the tank, as shown.

Wheels and wheel machinery

4

Treads

3. Add the wheels and more details along the tread and body of the tank. Erase guidelines as you go.

Note: It's easy to draw almost anything if you first build a good foundation.

4. Shade and refine the tank, as shown. Note the details at the end of the cannon, on the body and front of the tank, and along its wheels and treads.

U.S.S. CONSTITUTION

Also known as "Old Ironsides," the U.S.S. *Constitution* is the oldest ship in the U.S. Navy. This ship first set sail in 1798 and was instrumental in defeating the British during the War of 1812. It has 44 guns aboard and holds a crew of almost 500.

1. Start "Old Ironsides" by drawing a free-form shape for the body of the ship and long lines for the masts.

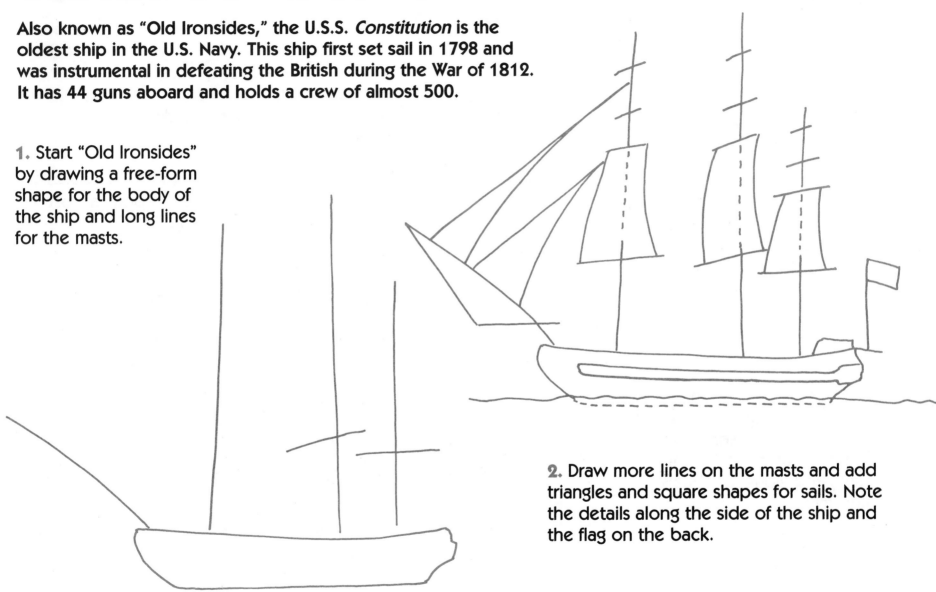

2. Draw more lines on the masts and add triangles and square shapes for sails. Note the details along the side of the ship and the flag on the back.

3. Further refine the sails and add circles to the front and side of the ship.

4. Draw in ropes between the sails and to the front of the ship. Add lines and shade the circles to show the cannons. "Old Ironsides" is ready for battle!

F-5E TIGER TURBO JET

This close-range fighter is more maneuverable than other fighter jets. It has deadly sidewinder missiles mounted on its wing tips, night-vision capabilities, and machine guns mounted in its nose.

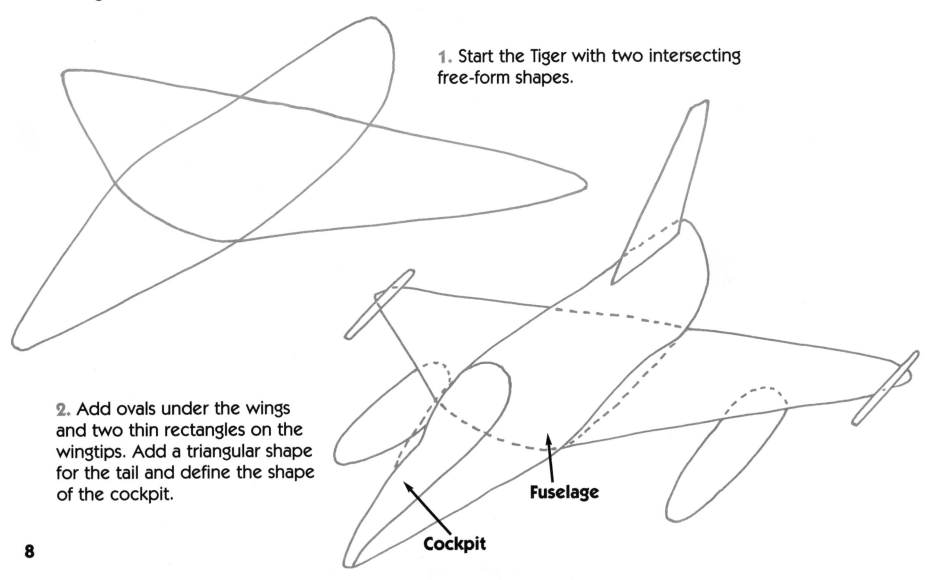

1. Start the Tiger with two intersecting free-form shapes.

2. Add ovals under the wings and two thin rectangles on the wingtips. Add a triangular shape for the tail and define the shape of the cockpit.

Fuselage

Cockpit

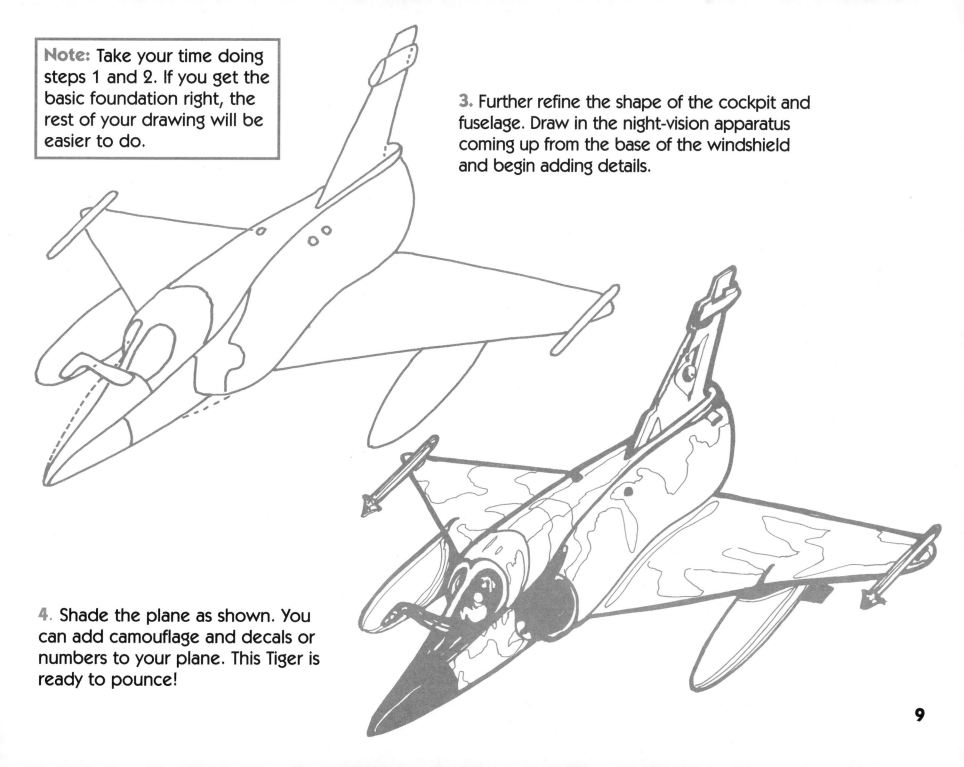

Note: Take your time doing steps 1 and 2. If you get the basic foundation right, the rest of your drawing will be easier to do.

3. Further refine the shape of the cockpit and fuselage. Draw in the night-vision apparatus coming up from the base of the windshield and begin adding details.

4. Shade the plane as shown. You can add camouflage and decals or numbers to your plane. This Tiger is ready to pounce!

U.S.S. ESSEX

This immense aircraft carrier began serving the U.S. Navy in 1942, during World War II. It remained in service until 1969.

Note: Always keep your pencil lines light and soft, so that the guidelines will be easier to erase when you no longer need them.

1. To launch the U.S.S. *Essex,* draw two free-form shapes: one for the deck of the ship, the other for the tower.

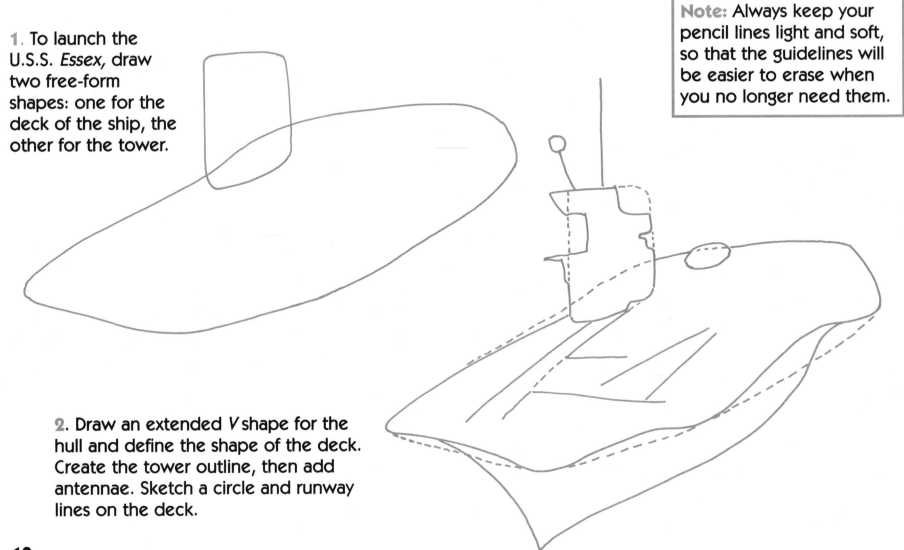

2. Draw an extended *V* shape for the hull and define the shape of the deck. Create the tower outline, then add antennae. Sketch a circle and runway lines on the deck.

3. Add the waterline, the helicopter outline, and other details on the deck. Continue to refine the tower, erasing guidelines as you go.

4. Add little sections and details to the tower. Draw planes and helicopters in the air or on the deck, and add all the finishing touches to complete your aircraft carrier.

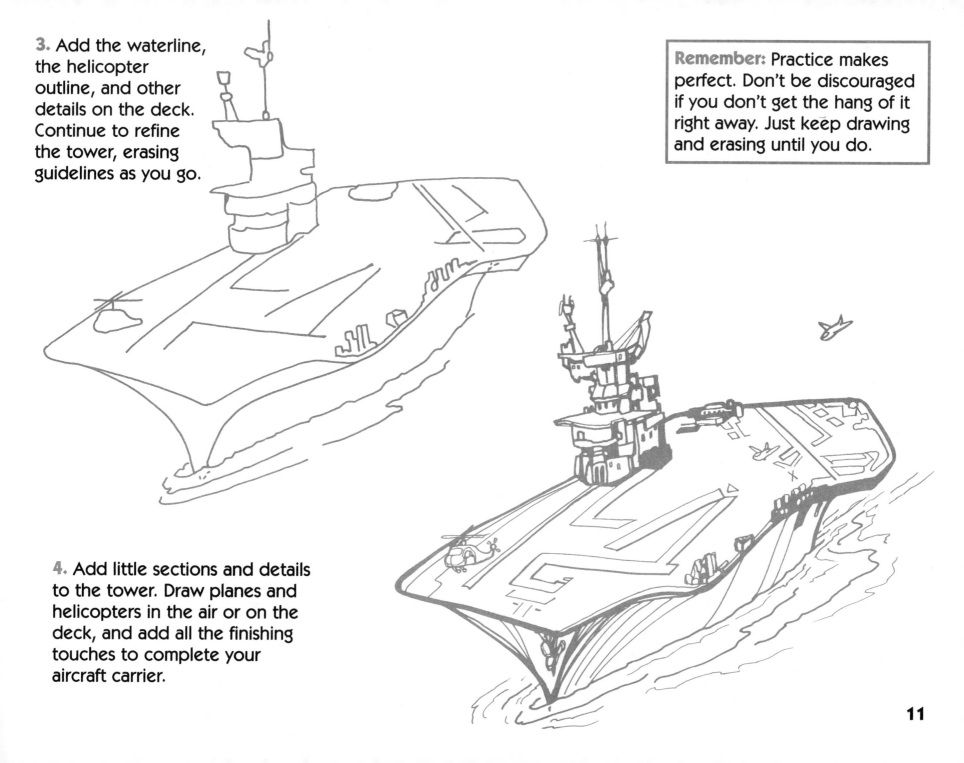

F-22 RAPTOR

The F-22 is the latest U.S. air-dominance fighter plane. It has a speed of Mach 2 and possesses a sophisticated sensor suite that allows its pilot to track, identify, and shoot a threat before being detected.

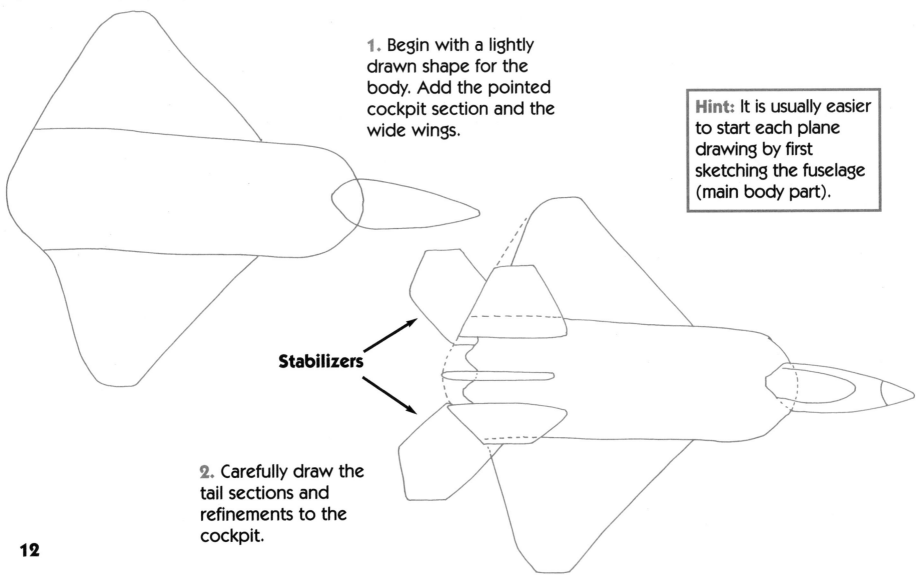

1. Begin with a lightly drawn shape for the body. Add the pointed cockpit section and the wide wings.

Hint: It is usually easier to start each plane drawing by first sketching the fuselage (main body part).

Stabilizers

2. Carefully draw the tail sections and refinements to the cockpit.

3. Complete the F-22's rear section, creating a double line around the tails and stabilizers and continuing along the edges of the wings. Add more small shapes to the front section.

4. Add lots of details: shading, camouflage lines, insignia, etc. Keep drawing and erasing until you are satisfied with the way your Raptor looks.

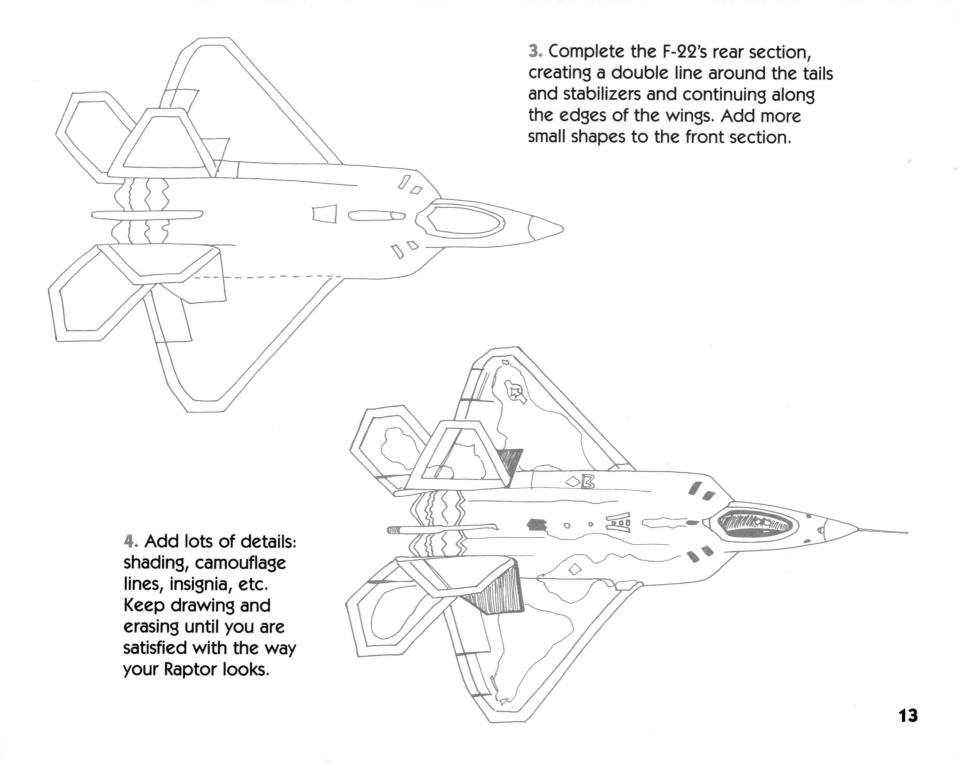

ABRAMS M-1 BATTLE TANK

This tank weighs 120,000 pounds and seats four crew members. With armor that is almost impossible to pierce, the Abrams tank has served the U.S. Army since 1978.

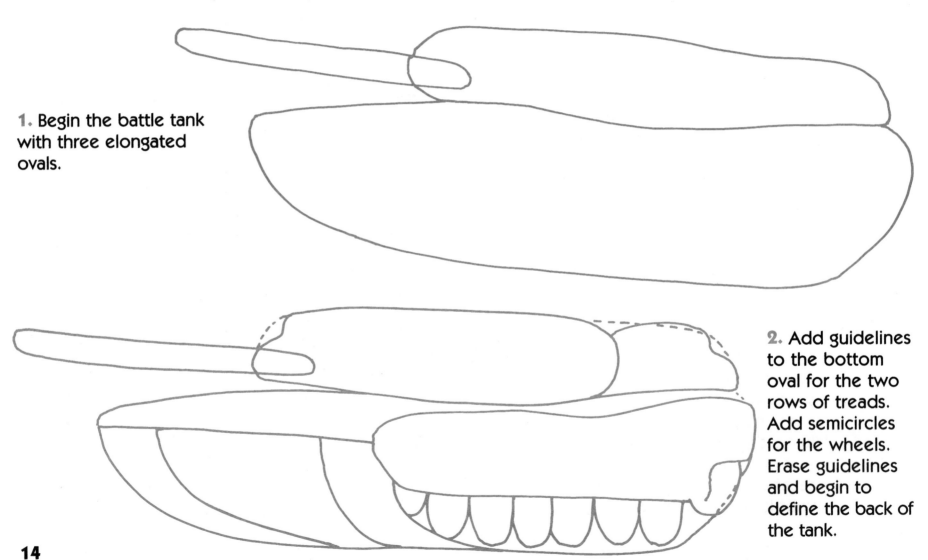

1. Begin the battle tank with three elongated ovals.

2. Add guidelines to the bottom oval for the two rows of treads. Add semicircles for the wheels. Erase guidelines and begin to define the back of the tank.

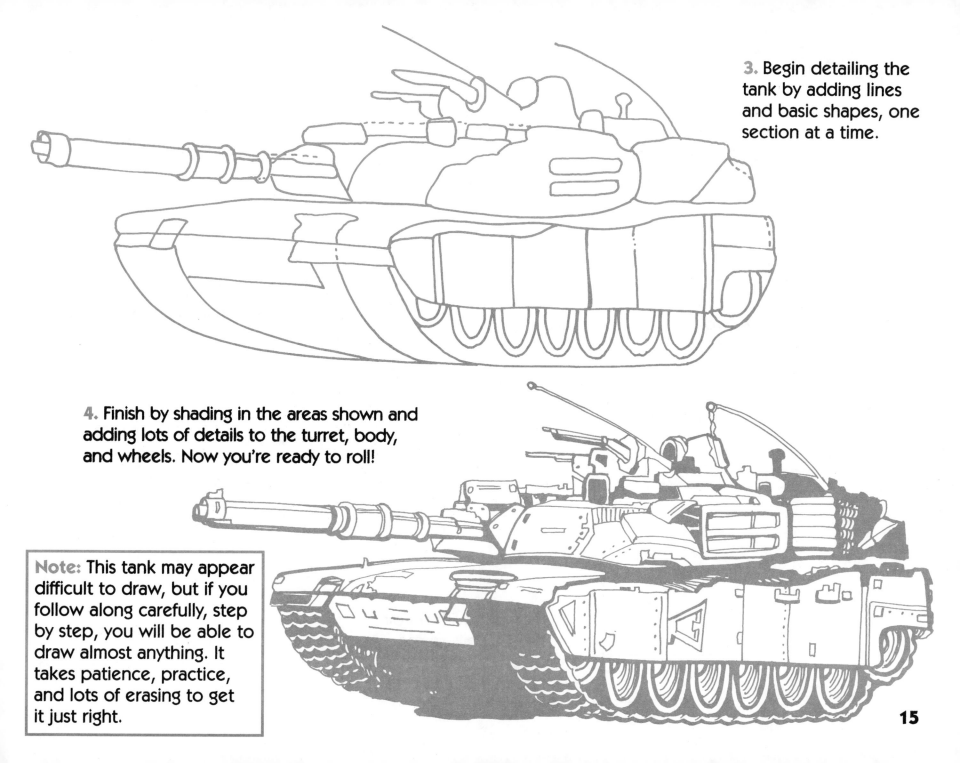

3. Begin detailing the tank by adding lines and basic shapes, one section at a time.

4. Finish by shading in the areas shown and adding lots of details to the turret, body, and wheels. Now you're ready to roll!

Note: This tank may appear difficult to draw, but if you follow along carefully, step by step, you will be able to draw almost anything. It takes patience, practice, and lots of erasing to get it just right.

XM-8 TANK

Used during Operation Desert Storm (the Persian Gulf War) in 1991, this tank has night-vision capabilities and four heat-seeking missiles that can engage targets in nearly all weather conditions.

2. Add curved shapes on either side of the top square to form the heat-seeking missiles. Draw in the details to the front end and begin refining the tires.

Hint: Add details and all the finishing touches *after* you have blended and refined the shapes and your figure is complete.

1. Begin this head-on view of the tank by stacking three rectangles to form the body. Draw two semi-circles on the bottom.

3. Finish with shading and details to the missiles, main cannon, front end, and tires.

U.S.S. NAUTILUS

The U.S.S. *Nautilus* was the world's first nuclear-powered submarine and the first submarine to cross the geographic North Pole. It has 6 torpedo tubes and can hold more than 100 crew members.

1. Begin the *Nautilus* by drawing a long, narrow oval with a square on top. Note the details added to one end of the oval.

Hint: At each step, keep erasing and drawing until you are satisfied with the way your drawing looks.

2. Start drawing the waterline and add the periscope to the top of the square. Draw the additional shapes on the front of the sub and begin adding details.

3. Add the final touches to the U.S.S. *Nautilus* as it prepares to dive!

17

U.S.S. ARIZONA

The U.S.S. *Arizona* is one of the most famous battleships in the U.S. Navy. It was sunk at Pearl Harbor during the Japanese invasion on December 7, 1941. Today, a memorial stands over the ship's sunken remains to honor all the crew members who lost their lives during the attack.

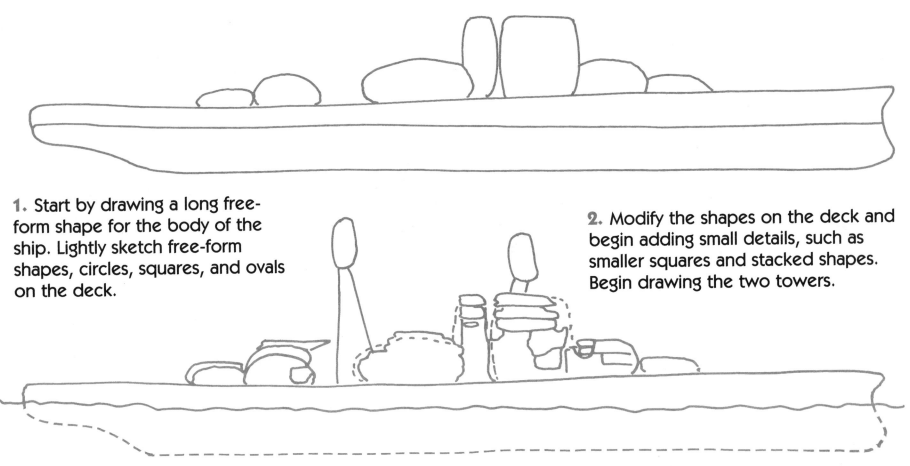

1. Start by drawing a long free-form shape for the body of the ship. Lightly sketch free-form shapes, circles, squares, and ovals on the deck.

2. Modify the shapes on the deck and begin adding small details, such as smaller squares and stacked shapes. Begin drawing the two towers.

Hint: Keep all your guidelines lightly drawn. They will be easier to erase later on.

3. Further detail the deck of the battleship. Add long, thin rectangular shapes facing forward and backward. Continue detailing the towers.

4. Finish the U.S.S. *Arizona* by adding details along the side of the ship. Refine the towers and the guns on deck. (Note the flag at the front of the ship.)

B-2 WARBIRD

This fighter was instrumental in protecting ground troops and destroying enemy weapons during World War II.

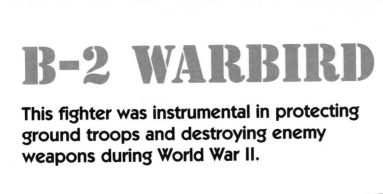

1. Begin with three intersecting free-form shapes.

2. Erase guidelines and add shapes for the tail sections and the cockpit.

> **Remember:** Always draw your guidelines lightly in steps 1 and 2. It will be easier to erase them later.

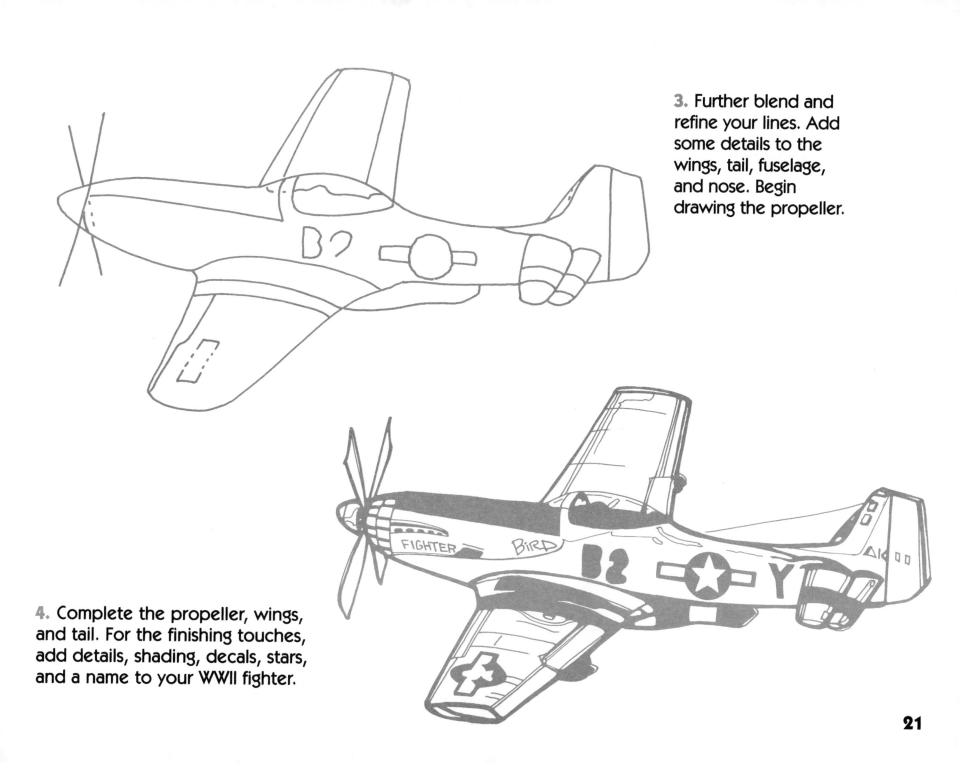

3. Further blend and refine your lines. Add some details to the wings, tail, fuselage, and nose. Begin drawing the propeller.

4. Complete the propeller, wings, and tail. For the finishing touches, add details, shading, decals, stars, and a name to your WWII fighter.

21

WORLD WAR I TANK

The tank was invented in 1916, during World War I. The protective guns and armor of tanks allowed soldiers to travel into enemy territory.

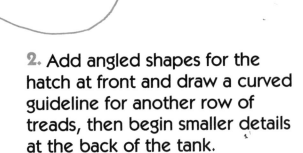

1. To begin, draw three overlapping ovals, as shown.

2. Add angled shapes for the hatch at front and draw a curved guideline for another row of treads, then begin smaller details at the back of the tank.

Remember: Take your time doing steps 1 and 2. If you get the basic foundation right, the rest of your drawing will be easy to do.

3. Create circles inside the tread and further refine the turret. Erase any guidelines you no longer need.

4. Shade and detail the tank. Show the wheels inside the tread and rivets in the armor. You can even add mud!

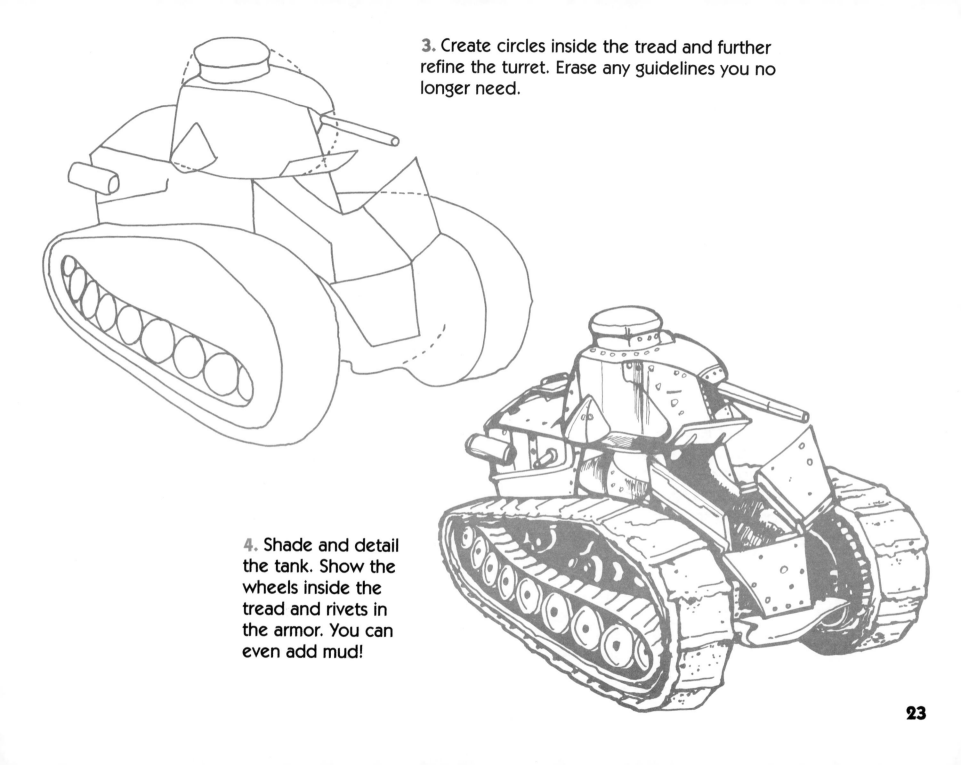

U-BOAT

German U-boats were submarines that could dive deep and travel quietly. They crippled U.S. and British shipping during WWI (1914-1919) and WWII (1939-1945).

1. Begin this deep-sea diver with a very long oval shape and two rounded shapes on top.

2. Draw lines to separate the deck from the body of the sub. Add more shapes to the deck and begin to add long, thin, rectangular shapes for the sub's guns, periscope, and snorkel (for taking in fresh air).

Hint: It's easy to draw almost anything if you first break it down into simple shapes.

3. Refine the on-deck gun and tower sections. Add more details to the front and back of the U-boat.

4. Continue adding details. When your drawing is complete, outline it with a black felt-tip pen. Add decals and a number for the final touch.

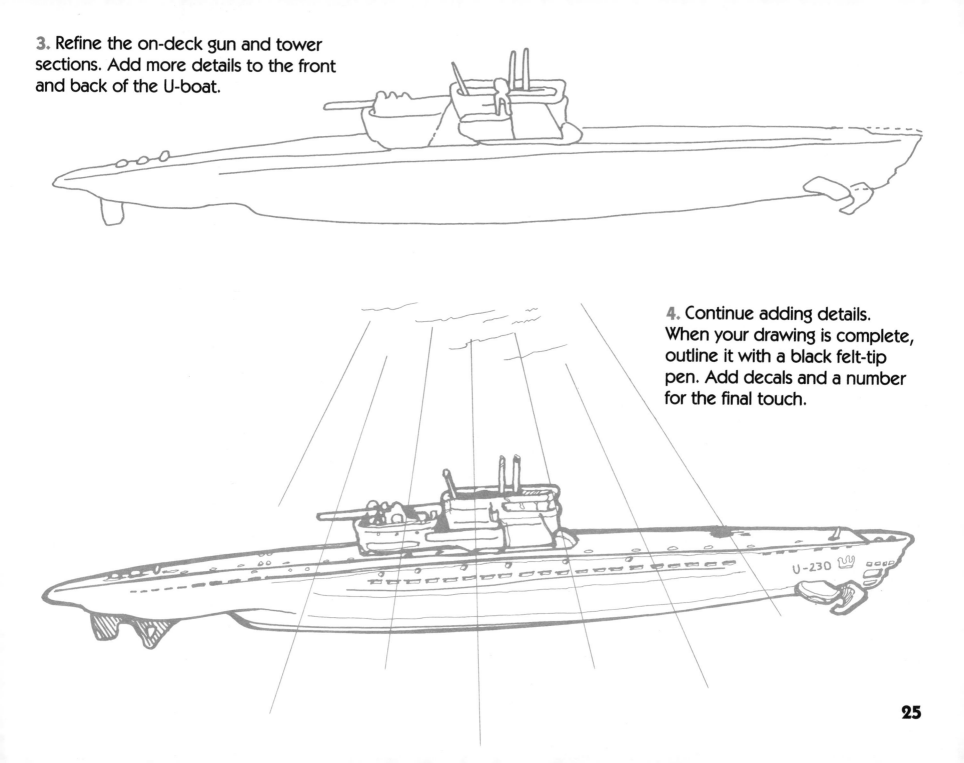

U-230

F-14 TOMCAT

The F-14 Tomcat is a swift and deadly fighter jet. It carries two crew members and can attack other planes in air-to-air combat or drop bombs on ground targets.

1. Begin your Tomcat with a loose free-form shape. Lightly draw in guidelines for the cockpit and tail fins.

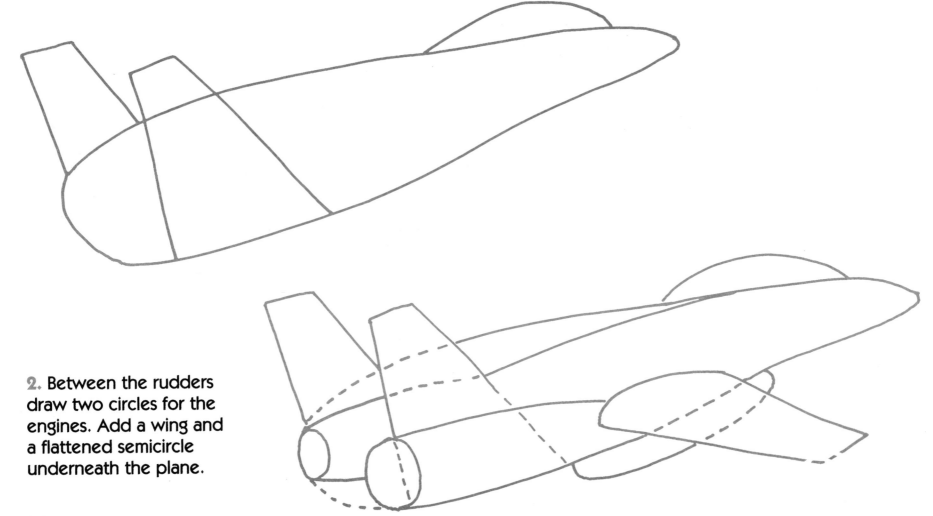

2. Between the rudders draw two circles for the engines. Add a wing and a flattened semicircle underneath the plane.

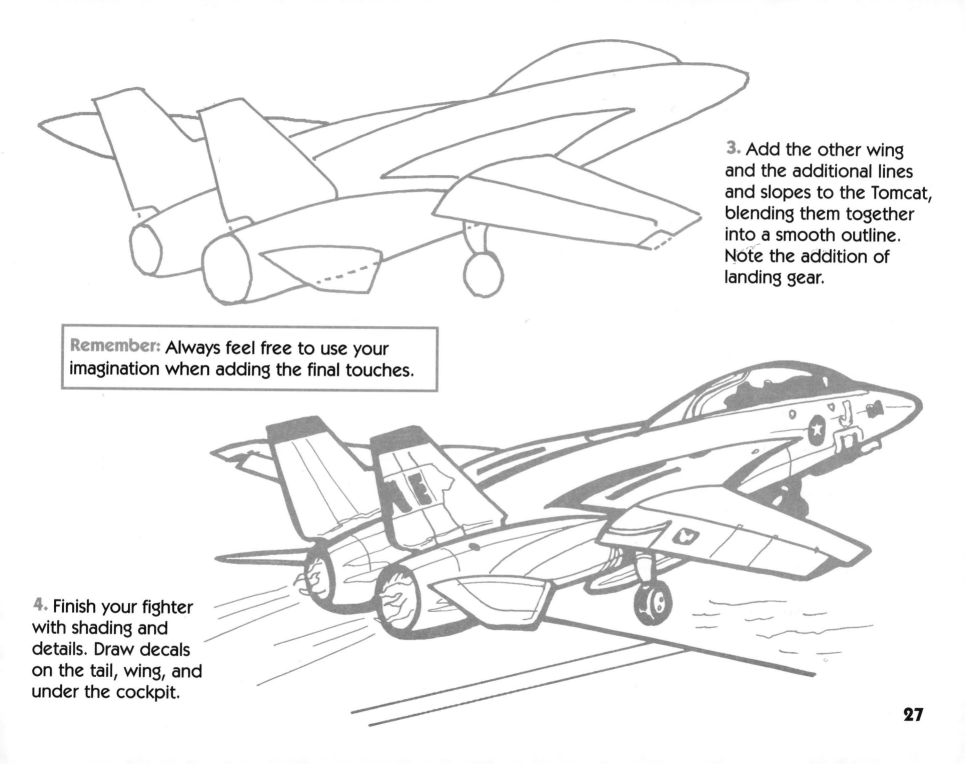

3. Add the other wing and the additional lines and slopes to the Tomcat, blending them together into a smooth outline. Note the addition of landing gear.

Remember: Always feel free to use your imagination when adding the final touches.

4. Finish your fighter with shading and details. Draw decals on the tail, wing, and under the cockpit.

27

CENTAURO TANK DESTROYER

This armored vehicle carries four people and can withstand even the harshest conditions. It fires armor-piercing rounds and has been used in peacekeeping missions around the world.

1. Begin with three large free-form shapes as shown.

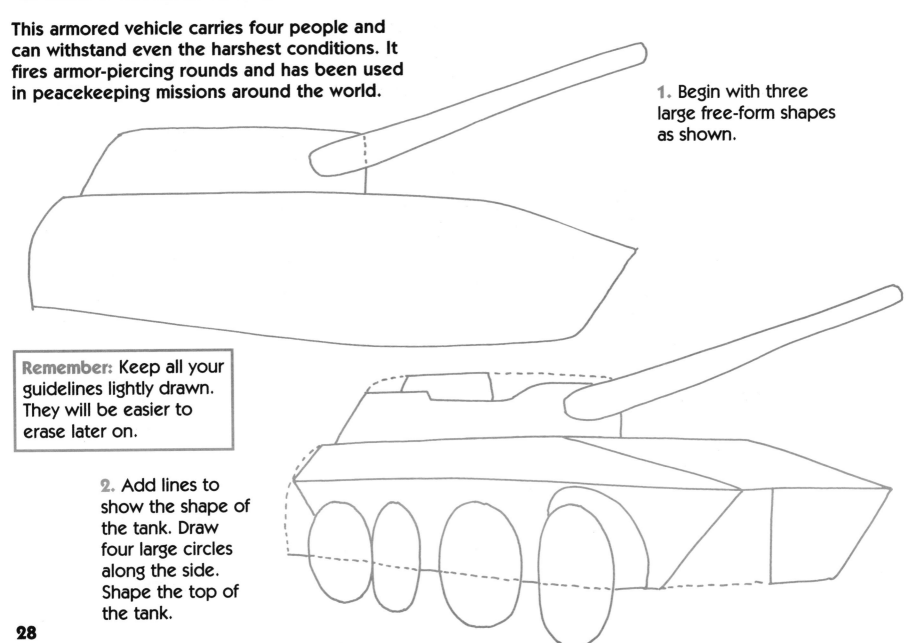

Remember: Keep all your guidelines lightly drawn. They will be easier to erase later on.

2. Add lines to show the shape of the tank. Draw four large circles along the side. Shape the top of the tank.

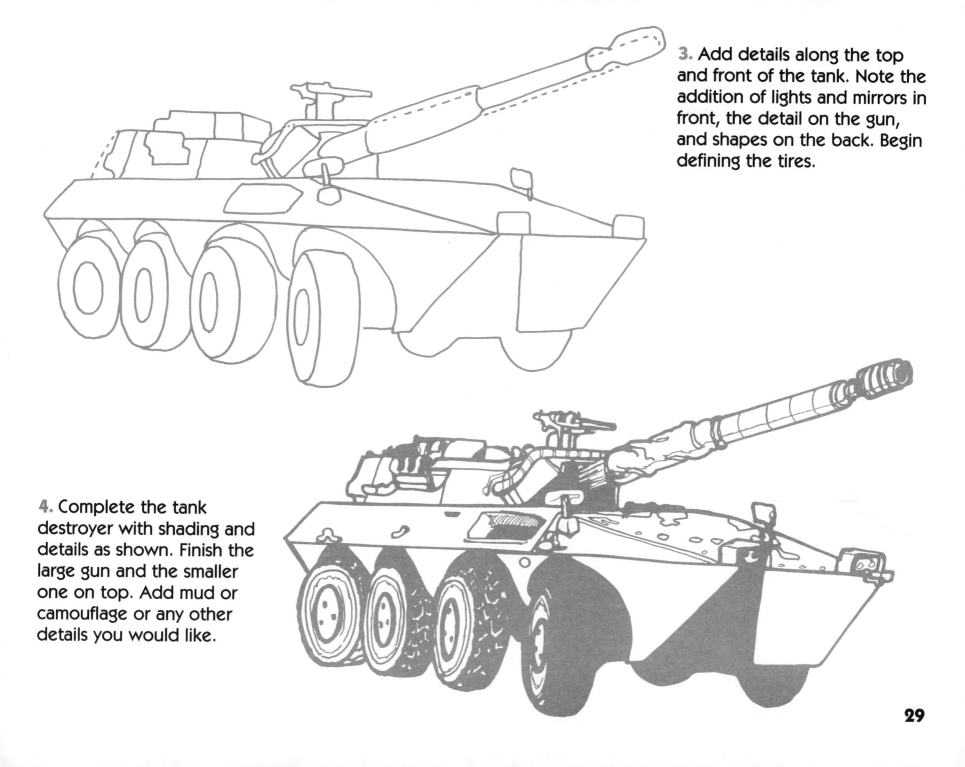

3. Add details along the top and front of the tank. Note the addition of lights and mirrors in front, the detail on the gun, and shapes on the back. Begin defining the tires.

4. Complete the tank destroyer with shading and details as shown. Finish the large gun and the smaller one on top. Add mud or camouflage or any other details you would like.

MINERVA

The Minerva started as a regular motorcar. During WWI, however, the Belgian army added heavy armored plates and a Hotchkiss machine gun, turning it into a tough military vehicle. Named for the Roman goddess of war, the four-ton Minerva helped Belgian and Dutch units withstand attacks by Germany's cavalry.

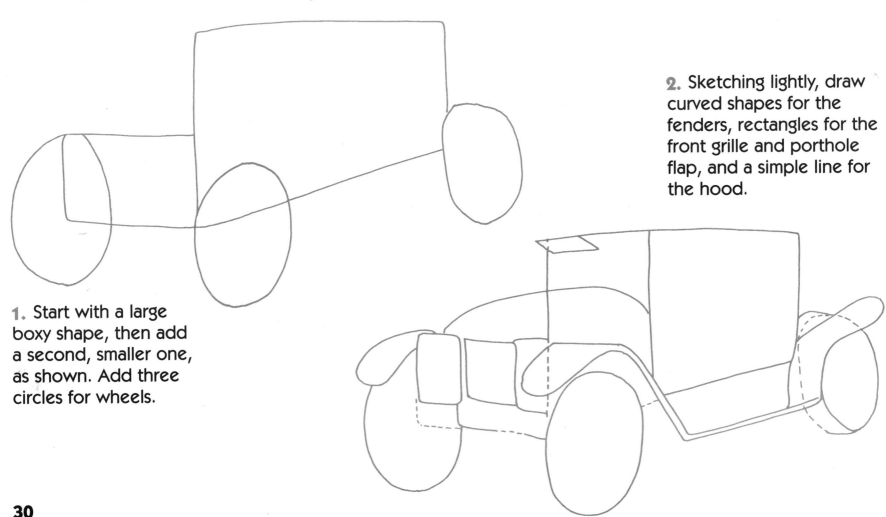

2. Sketching lightly, draw curved shapes for the fenders, rectangles for the front grille and porthole flap, and a simple line for the hood.

1. Start with a large boxy shape, then add a second, smaller one, as shown. Add three circles for wheels.

3. Draw a gun turret and guidelines for the gun, then add details to the body and wheels. Work on one section at a time until you are satisfied with it. Erase guidelines you no longer need.

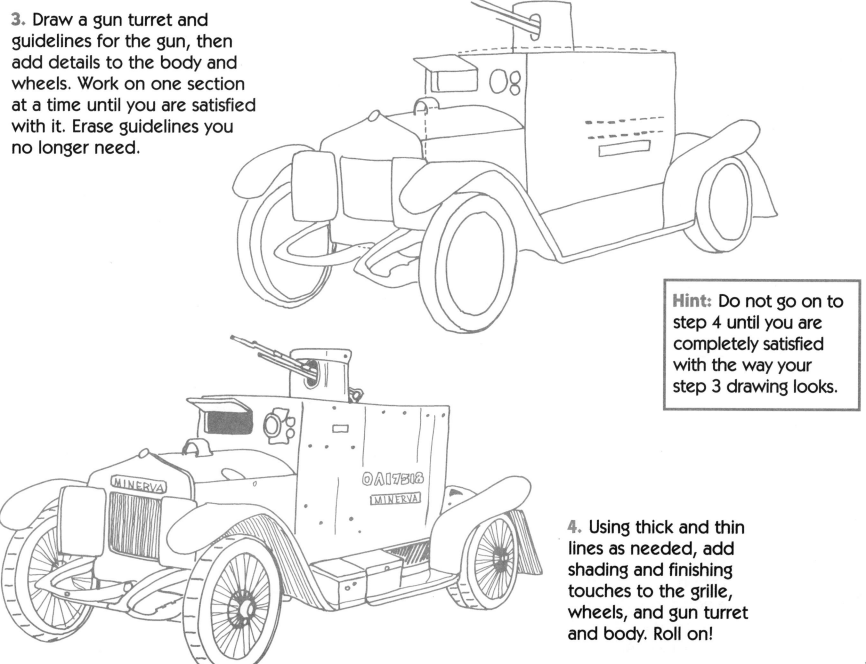

Hint: Do not go on to step 4 until you are completely satisfied with the way your step 3 drawing looks.

4. Using thick and thin lines as needed, add shading and finishing touches to the grille, wheels, and gun turret and body. Roll on!

31

FOKKER DR. I TRIPLANE

The nimble Dr. I earned a reputation as one of the best "dogfighters" of WWI. Manfred von Richthofen, the famed German pilot known as the Red Baron, scored 19 of his last 21 victories while flying the Dr. I.

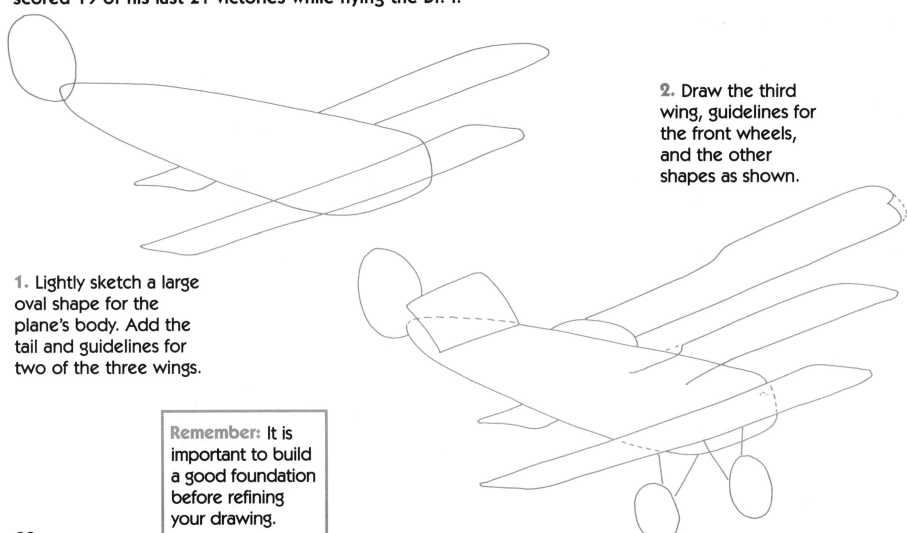

2. Draw the third wing, guidelines for the front wheels, and the other shapes as shown.

1. Lightly sketch a large oval shape for the plane's body. Add the tail and guidelines for two of the three wings.

Remember: It is important to build a good foundation before refining your drawing.

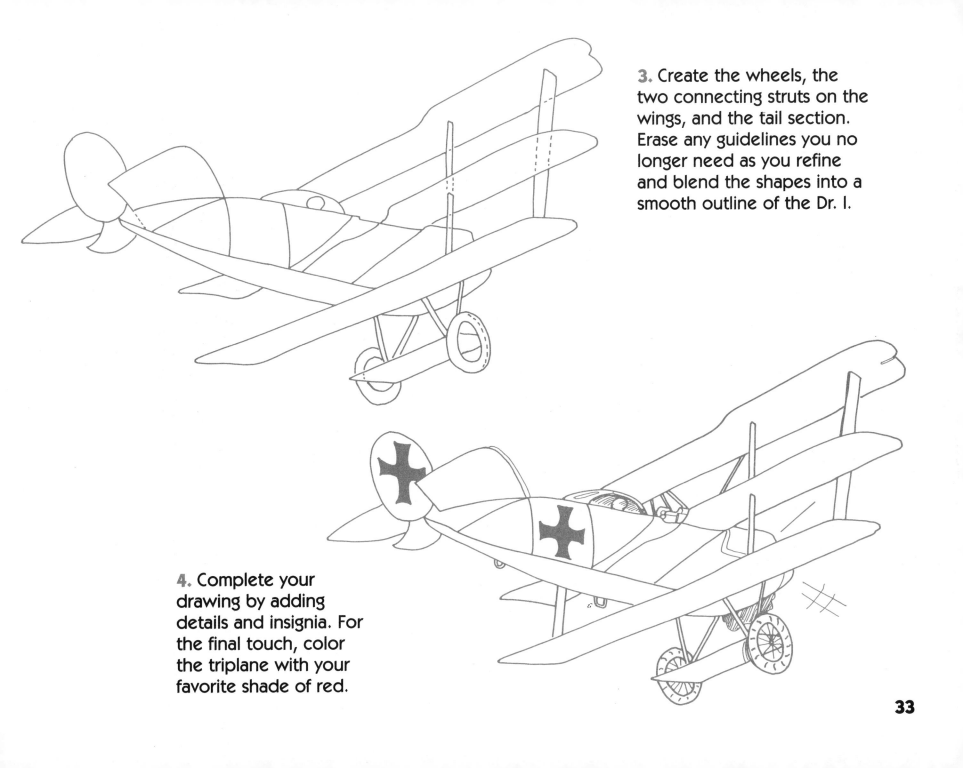

3. Create the wheels, the two connecting struts on the wings, and the tail section. Erase any guidelines you no longer need as you refine and blend the shapes into a smooth outline of the Dr. I.

4. Complete your drawing by adding details and insignia. For the final touch, color the triplane with your favorite shade of red.

BRDM-2 SCOUT CAR

The Russian BRDM-2 is an amphibious vehicle (one able to ride through water as well as on land). Its four-wheel drive belly wheels carry it across rough terrain, while its single waterjet propels it through water. Armed with two machine guns (a 14.5-mm and a 7.62-mm), it also has infrared driving lights and spotlight for night duty.

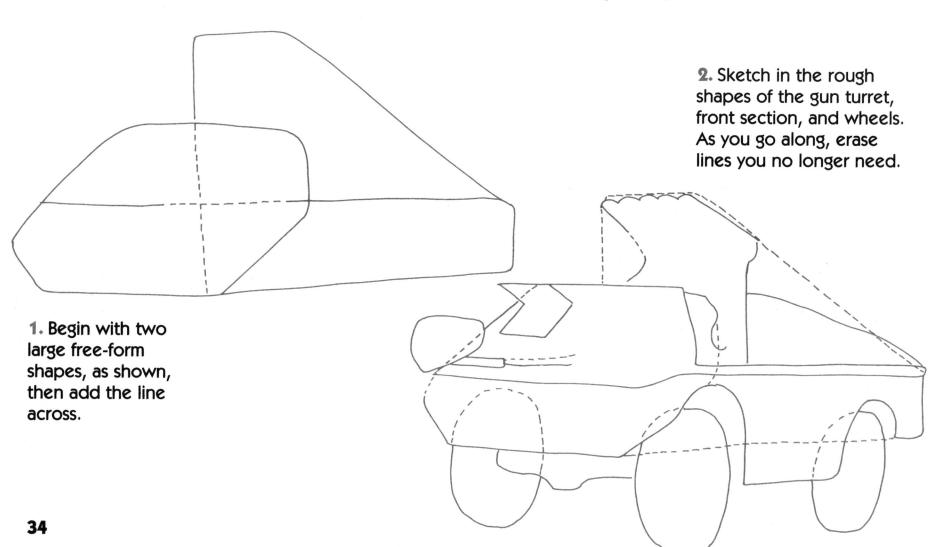

2. Sketch in the rough shapes of the gun turret, front section, and wheels. As you go along, erase lines you no longer need.

1. Begin with two large free-form shapes, as shown, then add the line across.

3. Add lines and shapes to bring out the details of the body (especially the front section and wheels) and gun turret. Work on one area at a time until you are satisfied with it.

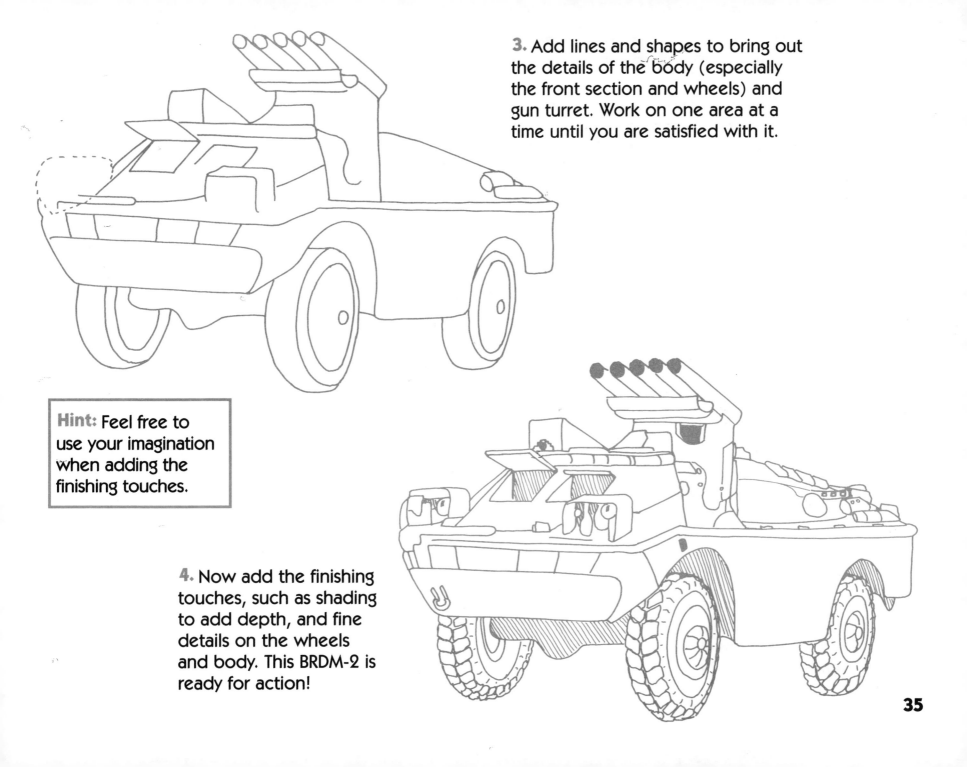

Hint: Feel free to use your imagination when adding the finishing touches.

4. Now add the finishing touches, such as shading to add depth, and fine details on the wheels and body. This BRDM-2 is ready for action!

T-80 BATTLE TANK

Produced by the Soviet Union in the 1980s, the T-80 is nick-named "Flying Tank" for a reason: It has a gas-turbine engine that enables it to move up to 43 mph. Its armaments include 125-mm, 12.7-mm, and 7.62-mm guns. The main gun can fire laser-guided rockets.

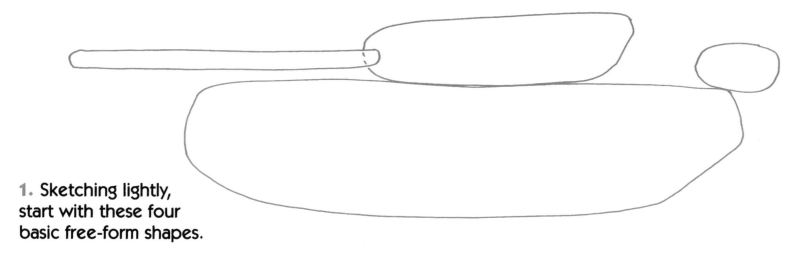

1. Sketching lightly, start with these four basic free-form shapes.

2. Add simple lines and shapes, as shown, to begin the wheels, treads, and basic body parts.

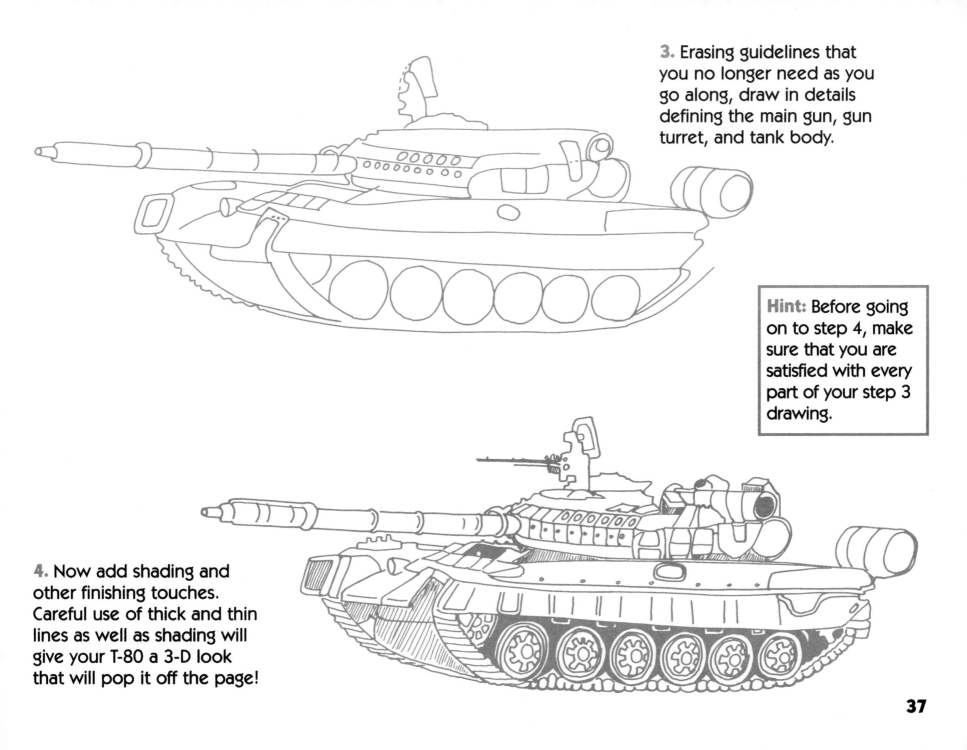

3. Erasing guidelines that you no longer need as you go along, draw in details defining the main gun, gun turret, and tank body.

Hint: Before going on to step 4, make sure that you are satisfied with every part of your step 3 drawing.

4. Now add shading and other finishing touches. Careful use of thick and thin lines as well as shading will give your T-80 a 3-D look that will pop it off the page!

37

S-37 BERKUT

The forward-swept wings of this Russian fighter jet, known as "the Golden Eagle," increase its maneuverability at high altitudes. It has a 30-mm cannon carrying 150 rounds of ammunition, as well as air-to-air and air-to-surface missiles.

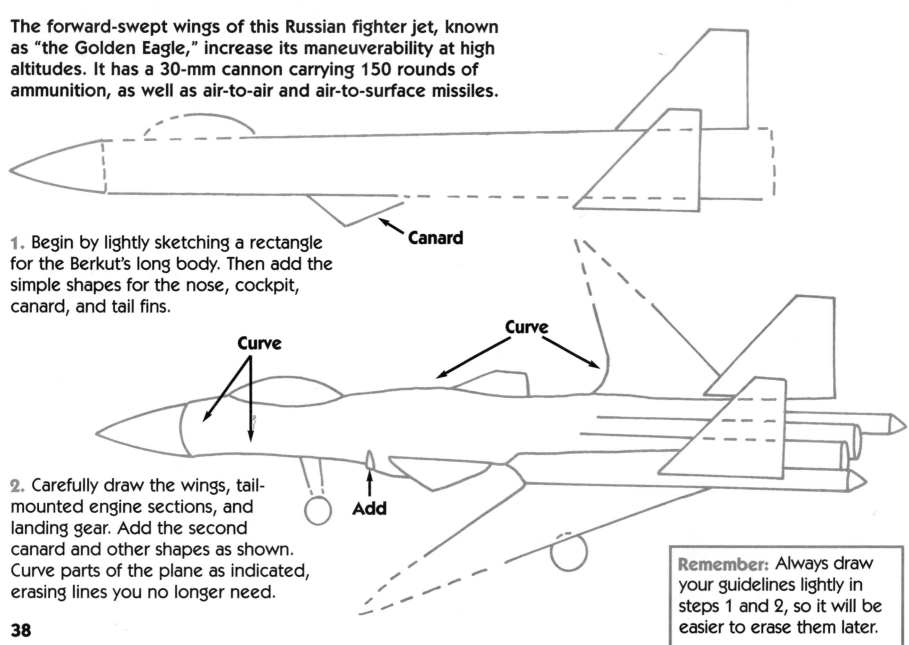

Canard

1. Begin by lightly sketching a rectangle for the Berkut's long body. Then add the simple shapes for the nose, cockpit, canard, and tail fins.

Curve

Curve

2. Carefully draw the wings, tail-mounted engine sections, and landing gear. Add the second canard and other shapes as shown. Curve parts of the plane as indicated, erasing lines you no longer need.

Add

Remember: Always draw your guidelines lightly in steps 1 and 2, so it will be easier to erase them later.

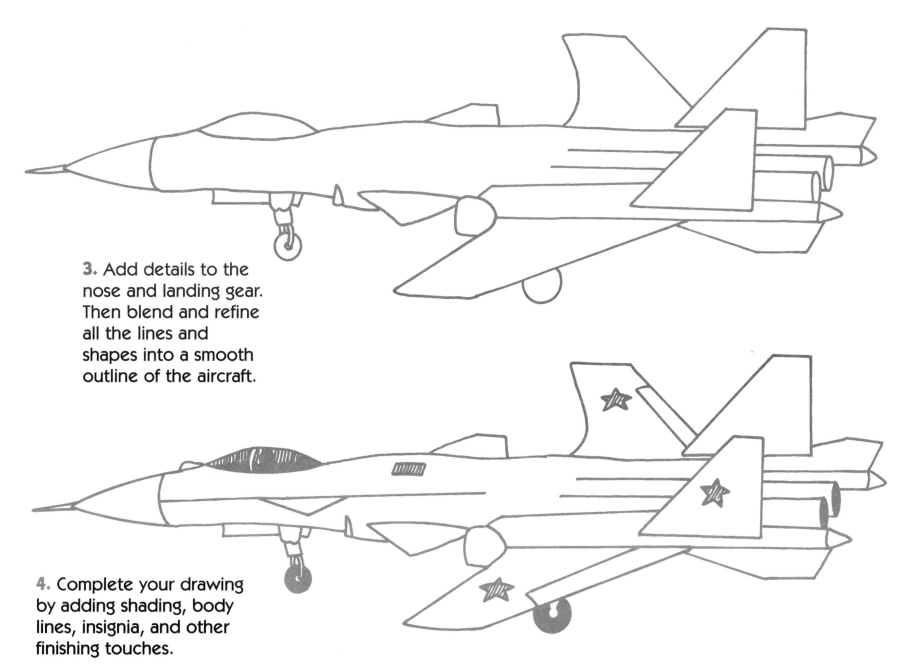

3. Add details to the nose and landing gear. Then blend and refine all the lines and shapes into a smooth outline of the aircraft.

4. Complete your drawing by adding shading, body lines, insignia, and other finishing touches.

BISMARCK

This immense German battleship, used during WWII, had a brief but intense life. Launched in 1939, its eight 15-inch guns and 30-knot speed terrorized the Allied fleet until 1941. After a fierce, all-night bombardment by British war-ships, the *Bismarck* sank on the morning of May 27, 1941.

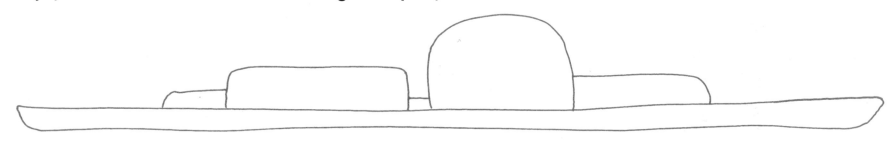

1. Start with a long, narrow shape, representing the ship's hull. Add simple lines and shapes for the craft's top sections, as shown.

2. Working within your step 1 guidelines, sketch in these smaller shapes to build the ship's top section. As you work, erase unneeded guidelines.

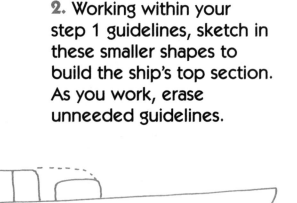

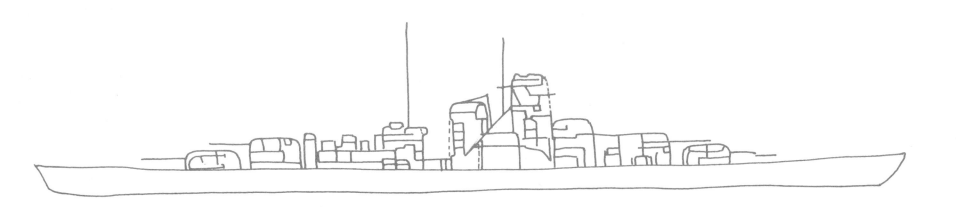

3. Using simple lines and shapes as shown, start breaking your basic top-section shapes into smaller, more detailed ones. Again, erase unneeded guidelines as you go.

Hint: This final drawing may look more difficult than most. If you take your time building a proper foundation in steps 1 and 2, however, the rest will be easy.

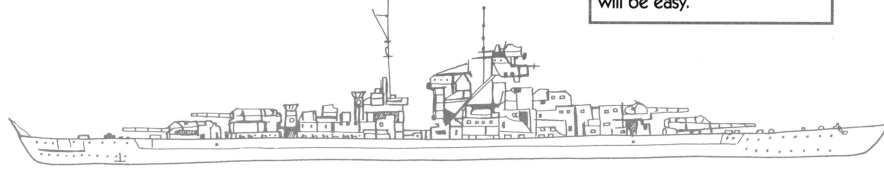

4. Only after you are completely satisfied with your step 3 drawing, add shading and other finishing touches. When you're done, this vessel will be truly seaworthy!

LVTP-7

This attack vehicle is amphibious: It can carry up to 25 Marines from their ships to the shore and on into a battle zone. (*LVTP* stands for landing vehicle tracked personnel.)

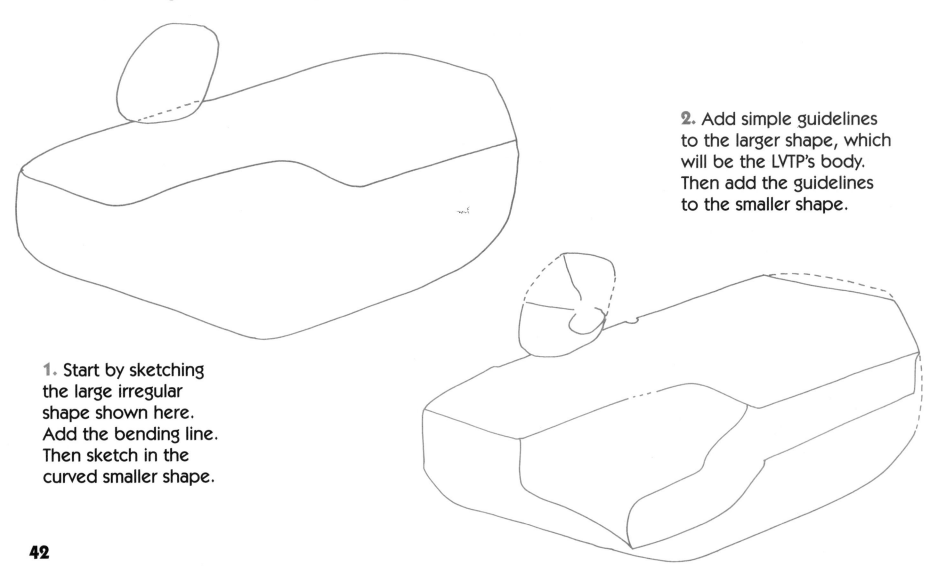

2. Add simple guidelines to the larger shape, which will be the LVTP's body. Then add the guidelines to the smaller shape.

1. Start by sketching the large irregular shape shown here. Add the bending line. Then sketch in the curved smaller shape.

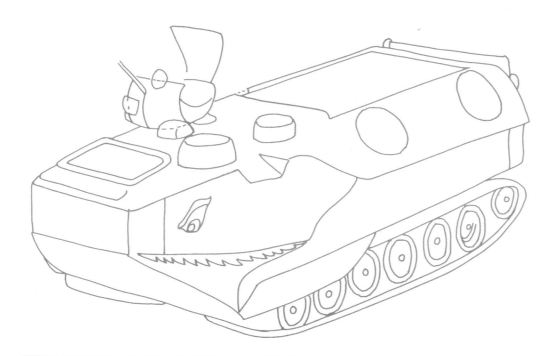

3. Begin sketching in details, as shown. Take your time with this step, working on just *one area at a time* until you are satisfied with it. As you go, erase guidelines you no longer need.

Note: Keep drawing and erasing until you are satisfied with the way your step 3 drawing looks. Don't go on to step 4 until step 3 is complete.

4. Now draw in the finishing touches. Use your imagination! Add a crew member or two, make the face as fierce as you like, or label your LVTP with a name of its own.

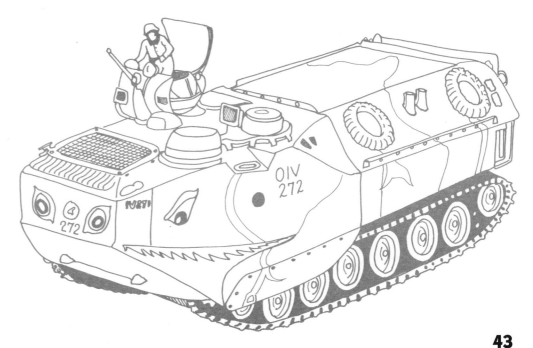

AVENGER

Developed in the 1980s, Avenger was designed to meet the U.S. Army's need for a shoot-on-the-move air-defense system. Each tough, lightweight vehicle carries eight surface-to-air Stinger missiles in two missile pods.

1. Start by sketching the large, free-form shape for the body. Add simple shapes as guidelines for the wheels, windshield, and first missile pod.

2. Draw simple lines to create the gun turret. Then add, adjust, or erase lines as needed to start giving shape to the front grille, missile pod, and wheels.

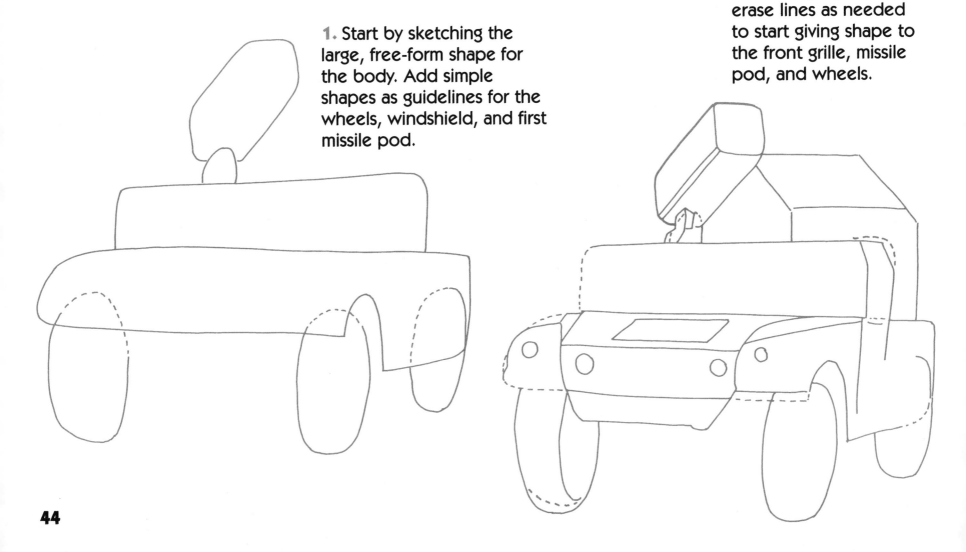

3. Add the second missile pod, then begin filling in details as shown, including guidelines and shapes for windshield wipers, rearview mirrors, and the front grille.

Remember: Always keep your pencil lines light and soft, so they will be easier to erase later on.

4. Smooth and blend all lines for a clean outline, then add the finishing touches. Careful use of shading will add depth—and drama.

ZERO (A6M REISEN)

The Japanese Zero was the finest shipboard fighter plane in the Pacific during the first year of WWII. It became legendary in its own time for its extremely good maneuverability and exceptionally long range (of almost 2,000 miles).

Remember: Steps 1 and 2 are very important. They establish the overall structure and look of your drawing.

1. Begin with a long carrot-shaped oval for the body. Add the wings and a circle on the side of the fuselage.

2. Draw the tail section, the canopy over the cockpit, a curved line defining the engine, and circles on the wings.

46

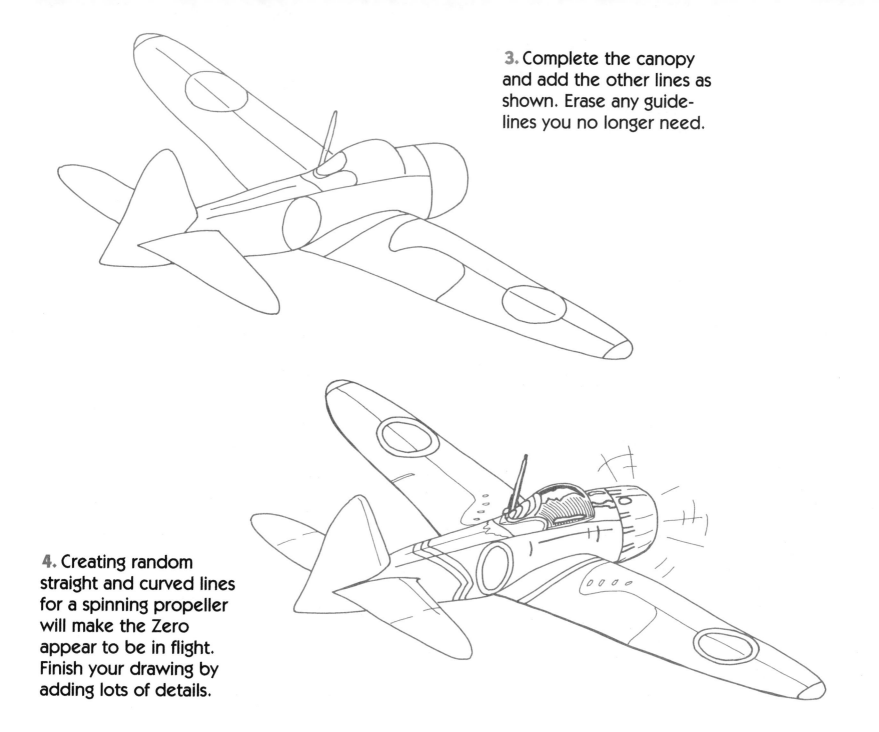

3. Complete the canopy and add the other lines as shown. Erase any guidelines you no longer need.

4. Creating random straight and curved lines for a spinning propeller will make the Zero appear to be in flight. Finish your drawing by adding lots of details.

BRADLEY TANK

Large but swift, the Bradley can move over sand, mud, water, or almost any type of terrain. Its main weapon is a 25-mm Bushmaster chain gun able to fire 200-500 rounds per minute. It also has smoke-grenade launchers, a twin-tube launcher for antitank TOW missiles, and other weaponry. It has a three- to five-member crew with room for up to six infantry.

1. Begin with the two free-form shapes as shown. (Draw the larger one first.)

2. Draw a small oval at the top of the smaller shape and modify the shape as shown. Add rectangles next to the turret and half circles to start the wheels.

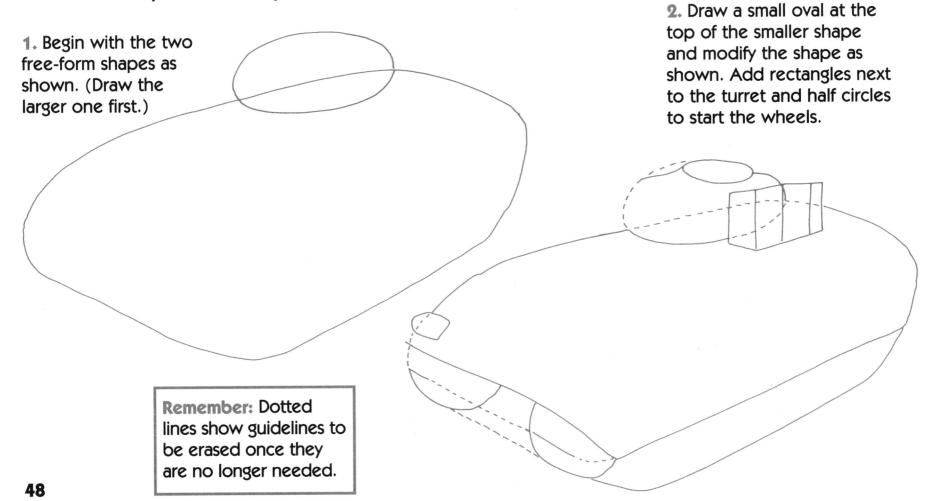

Remember: Dotted lines show guidelines to be erased once they are no longer needed.

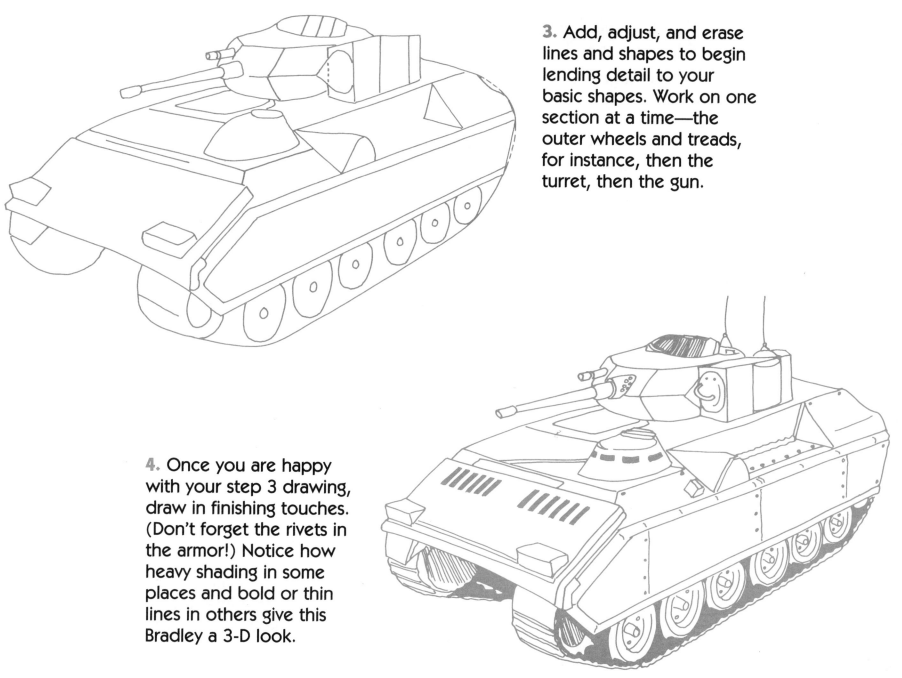

3. Add, adjust, and erase lines and shapes to begin lending detail to your basic shapes. Work on one section at a time—the outer wheels and treads, for instance, then the turret, then the gun.

4. Once you are happy with your step 3 drawing, draw in finishing touches. (Don't forget the rivets in the armor!) Notice how heavy shading in some places and bold or thin lines in others give this Bradley a 3-D look.

HMMV (HUMVEE)

HMMV stands for "high-mobility multipurpose vehicle," and the name suits it well. Known as the Humvee or Hummer, it is used by all branches of the U.S. armed forces in times of war and peace. It can be fitted with weaponry or firefighting equipment, for example, or set up as an ambulance, ammunition or cargo carrier, communications center, and so on.

1. Start by sketching these five free-form shapes. (Draw the largest one first.)

2. Sketching lightly, draw these simple lines and shapes to start the windows, rearview mirror, front end, and gun. Erase any unnecessary guidelines.

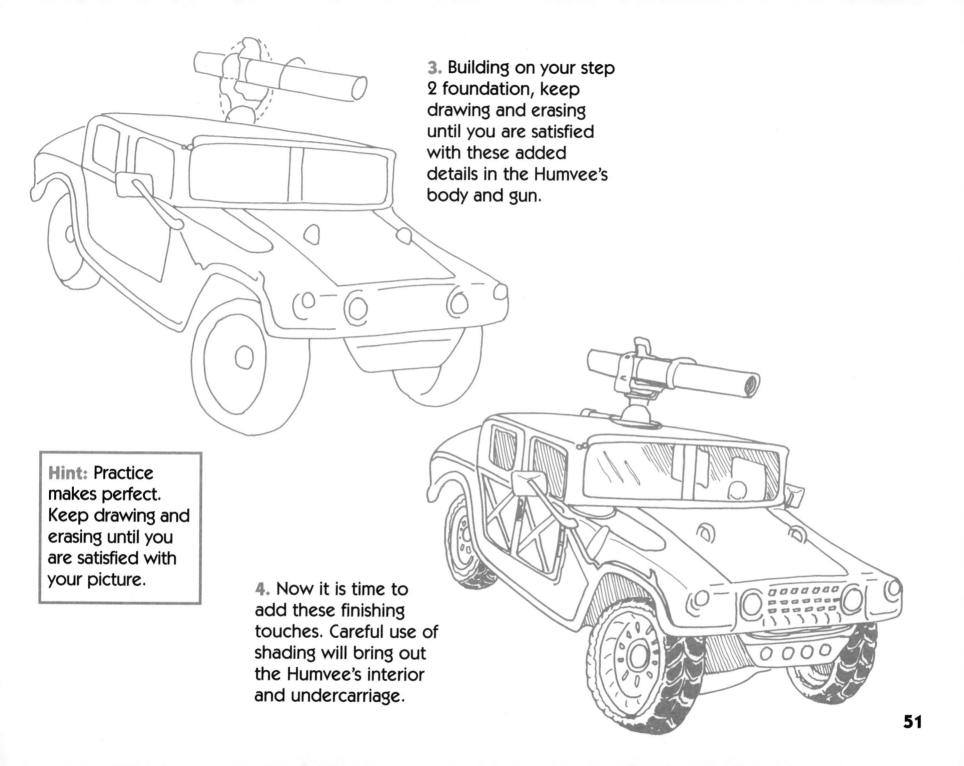

3. Building on your step 2 foundation, keep drawing and erasing until you are satisfied with these added details in the Humvee's body and gun.

Hint: Practice makes perfect. Keep drawing and erasing until you are satisfied with your picture.

4. Now it is time to add these finishing touches. Careful use of shading will bring out the Humvee's interior and undercarriage.

51

X-45A UCAV (UNMANNED COMBAT AIR VEHICLE)

The X-45A is a pilotless airborne robot that can snoop on adversaries and, if needed, deliver a knockout blow of bombs and missiles, all without risking the life of a pilot. Only 27 feet long with a 34-foot wingspan, this spy plane can be stored in small containers and assembled in about one hour.

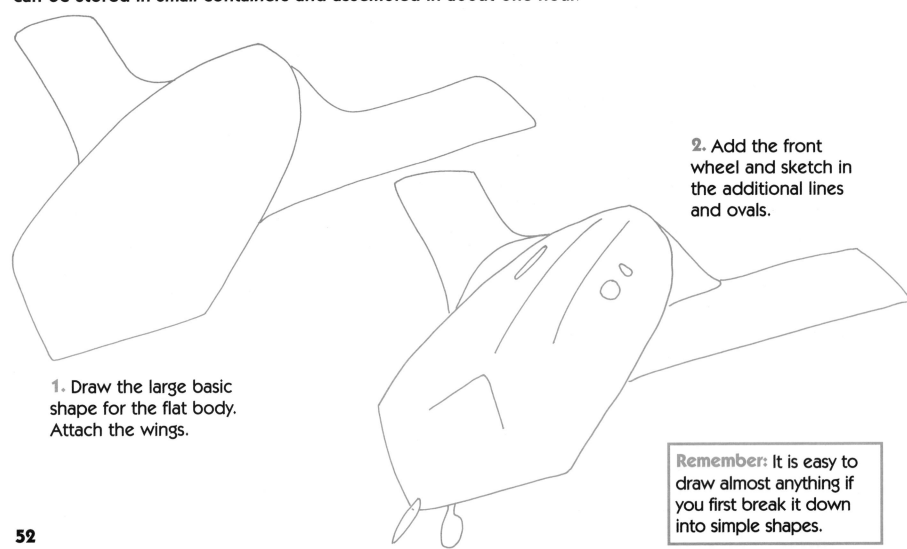

2. Add the front wheel and sketch in the additional lines and ovals.

1. Draw the large basic shape for the flat body. Attach the wings.

Remember: It is easy to draw almost anything if you first break it down into simple shapes.

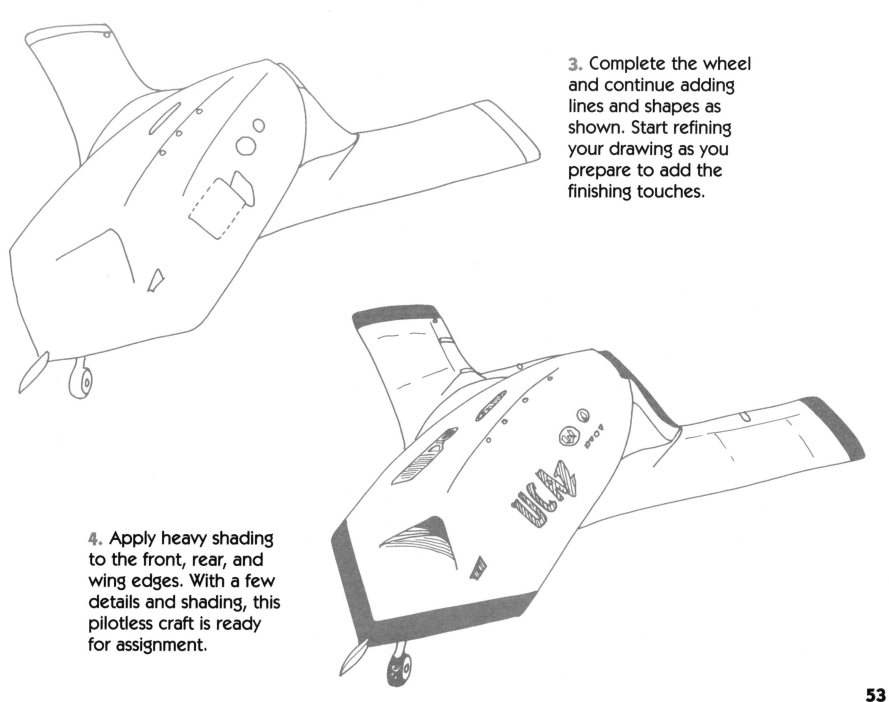

3. Complete the wheel and continue adding lines and shapes as shown. Start refining your drawing as you prepare to add the finishing touches.

4. Apply heavy shading to the front, rear, and wing edges. With a few details and shading, this pilotless craft is ready for assignment.

DESTROYER

A U.S. destroyer like this one may have one or two big guns and an arsenal of antiship missiles, surface-to-air missiles, and torpedoes for striking submarines. Many carry sub-hunter helicopters as well.

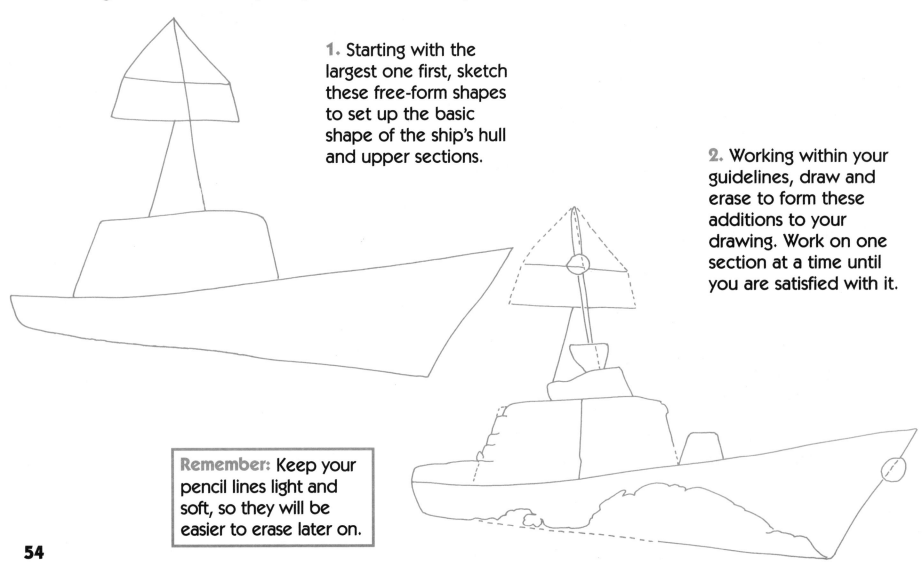

1. Starting with the largest one first, sketch these free-form shapes to set up the basic shape of the ship's hull and upper sections.

2. Working within your guidelines, draw and erase to form these additions to your drawing. Work on one section at a time until you are satisfied with it.

Remember: Keep your pencil lines light and soft, so they will be easier to erase later on.

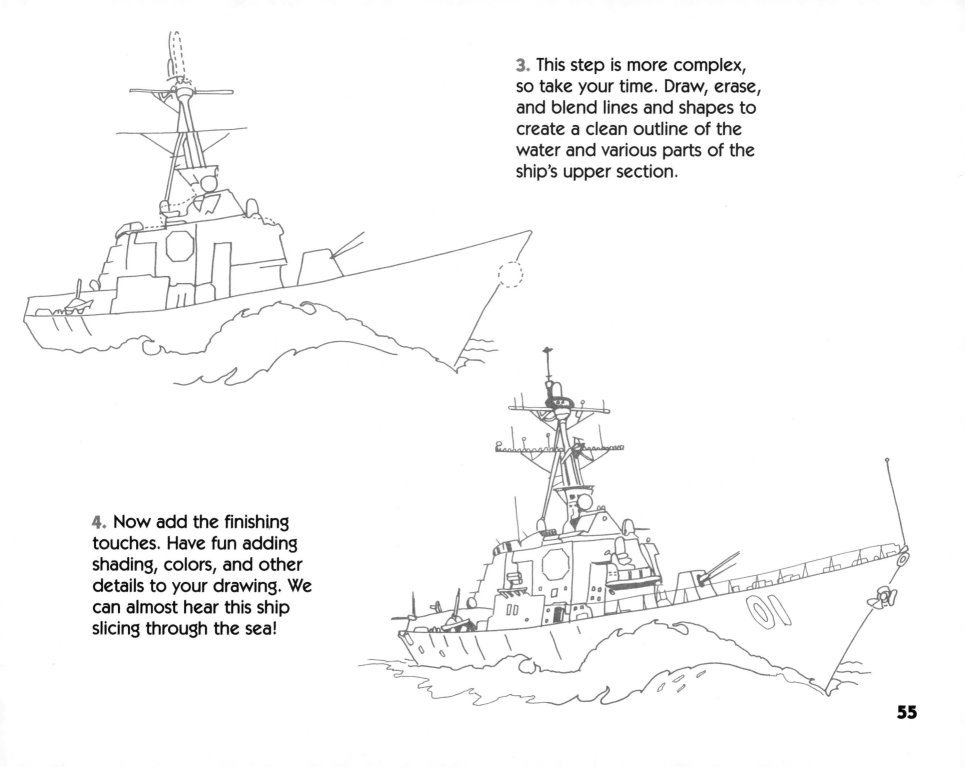

3. This step is more complex, so take your time. Draw, erase, and blend lines and shapes to create a clean outline of the water and various parts of the ship's upper section.

4. Now add the finishing touches. Have fun adding shading, colors, and other details to your drawing. We can almost hear this ship slicing through the sea!

PENNINGTON'S INVENTION

In 1896, E. J. Pennington, an American inventor, came up with this design for a battle vehicle: three machine guns on wheels, protected by metal plates. Like most of his ideas—including an airship, electric railway, and "cycle motor"—this one never went anywhere. However, later inventors came up with successful machines along similar lines.

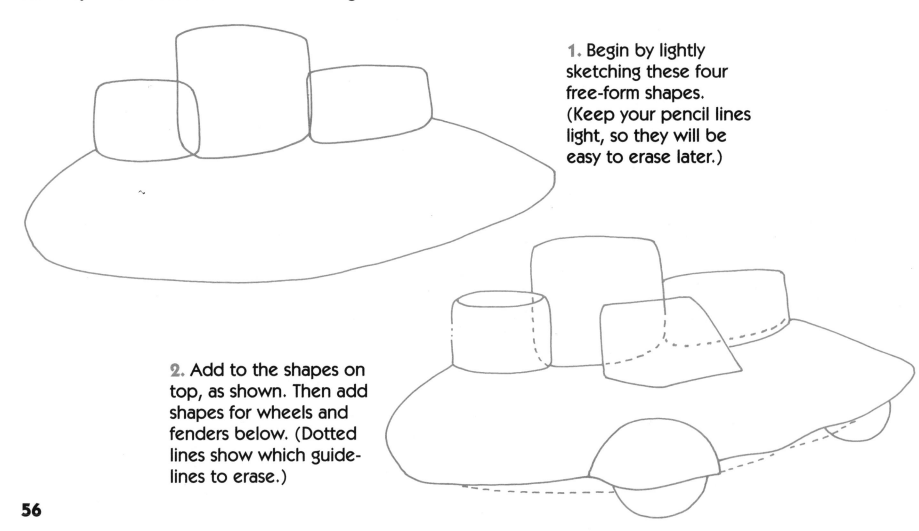

1. Begin by lightly sketching these four free-form shapes. (Keep your pencil lines light, so they will be easy to erase later.)

2. Add to the shapes on top, as shown. Then add shapes for wheels and fenders below. (Dotted lines show which guidelines to erase.)

3. Add, adjust, and erase to form the basic shapes of the gunners' shields and lightly sketch lines for the armor-plate seams. Draw rectangles for portholes, then add lines to define the wheels and fenders.

Hint: Add shading and other details only *after* you have blended and refined the shapes and your basic drawing is complete.

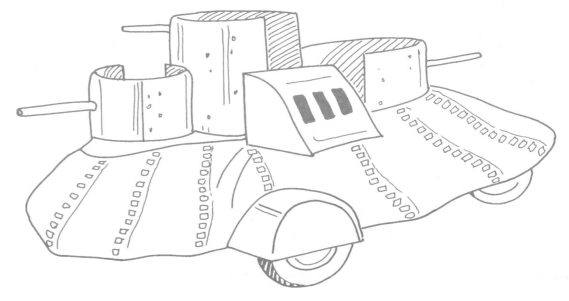

4. Add the finishing touches, such as rivets in the armor and shading to add depth. Color it, if you like. (Khaki? Camouflage? Use your imagination!)

2S1 SP HOWITZER

This Russian-built fighting machine—also called a Gvozdika SO-122—was the first amphibious, self-propelled artillery gun. (*SP* stands for "self-propelled"; a *howitzer* is a type of short cannon.) The height of this tough little vehicle can be adjusted for various situations, and its extra-wide track takes it over snow and swampland alike. It can carry up to 40 rounds of 122-mm ammunition.

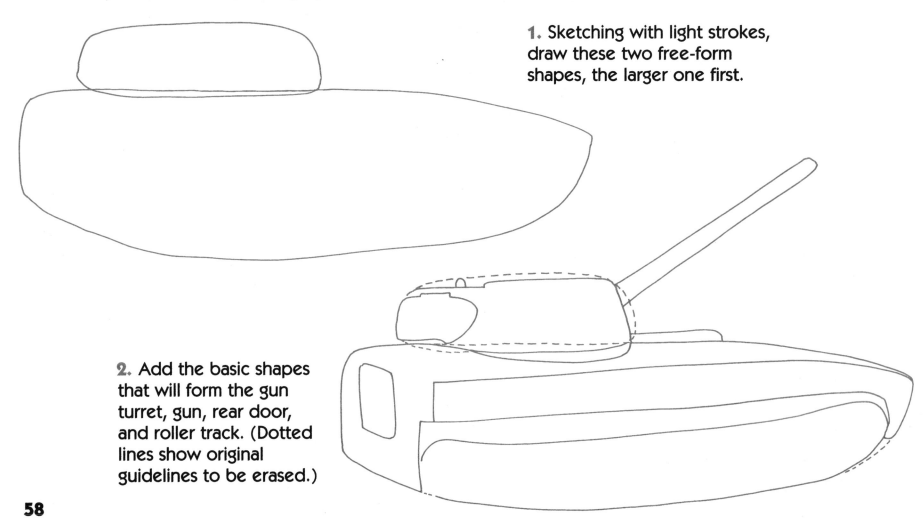

1. Sketching with light strokes, draw these two free-form shapes, the larger one first.

2. Add the basic shapes that will form the gun turret, gun, rear door, and roller track. (Dotted lines show original guidelines to be erased.)

3. Working carefully in one area at a time, draw, erase, and redraw until you are satisfied with everything being added in this step, such as the wheels and parts of the turret and gun.

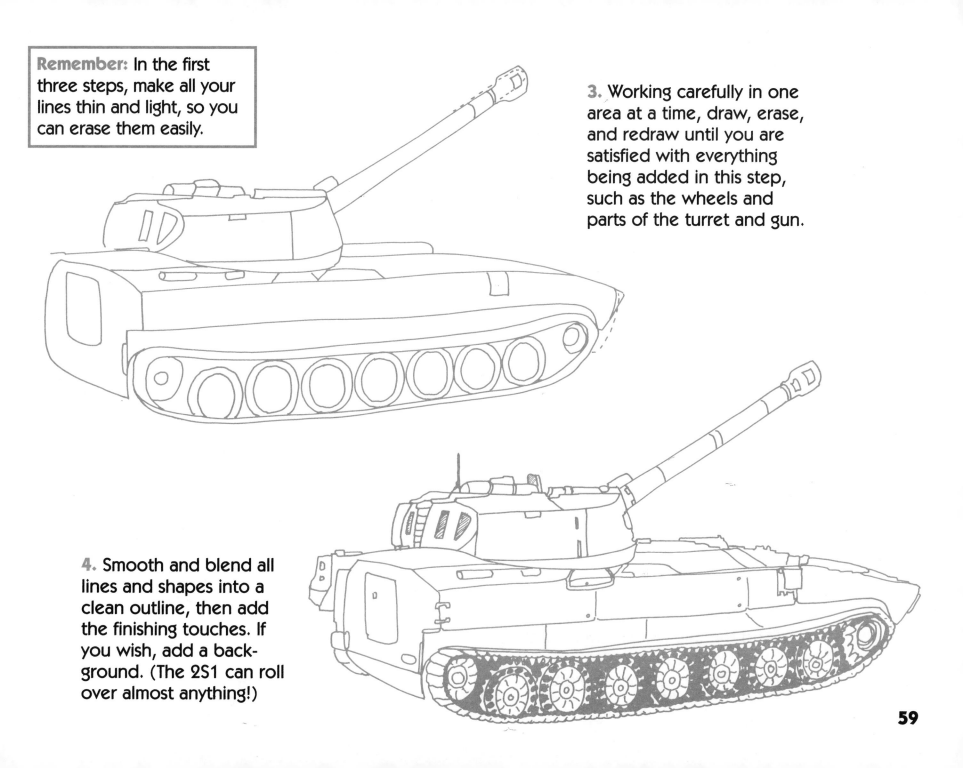

4. Smooth and blend all lines and shapes into a clean outline, then add the finishing touches. If you wish, add a background. (The 2S1 can roll over almost anything!)

JUNKERS Ju-87 STUKA

The most famous German WWII dive bomber was the Ju-87, nicknamed Stuka. Its wheel covers were fitted with sirens that turned on when the plane went into a dive—a sound meant to shatter the morale of enemy troops.

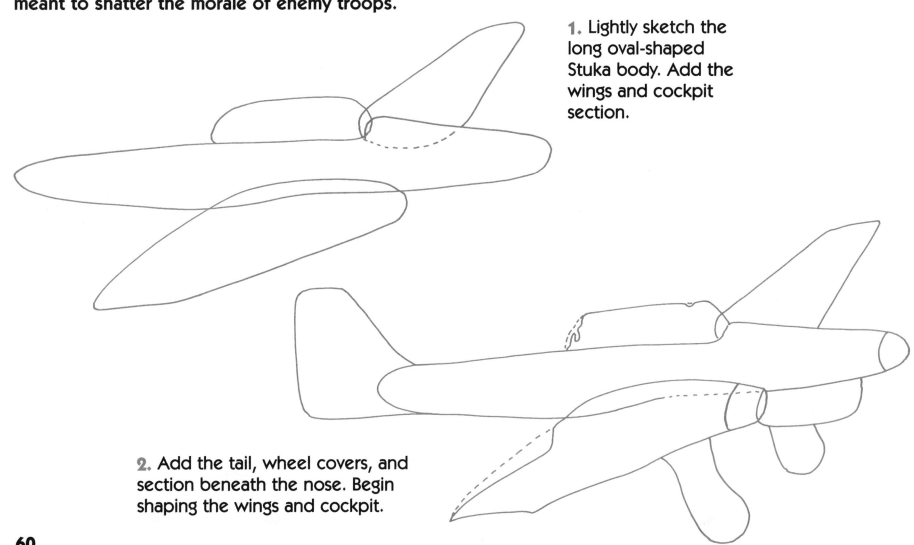

1. Lightly sketch the long oval-shaped Stuka body. Add the wings and cockpit section.

2. Add the tail, wheel covers, and section beneath the nose. Begin shaping the wings and cockpit.

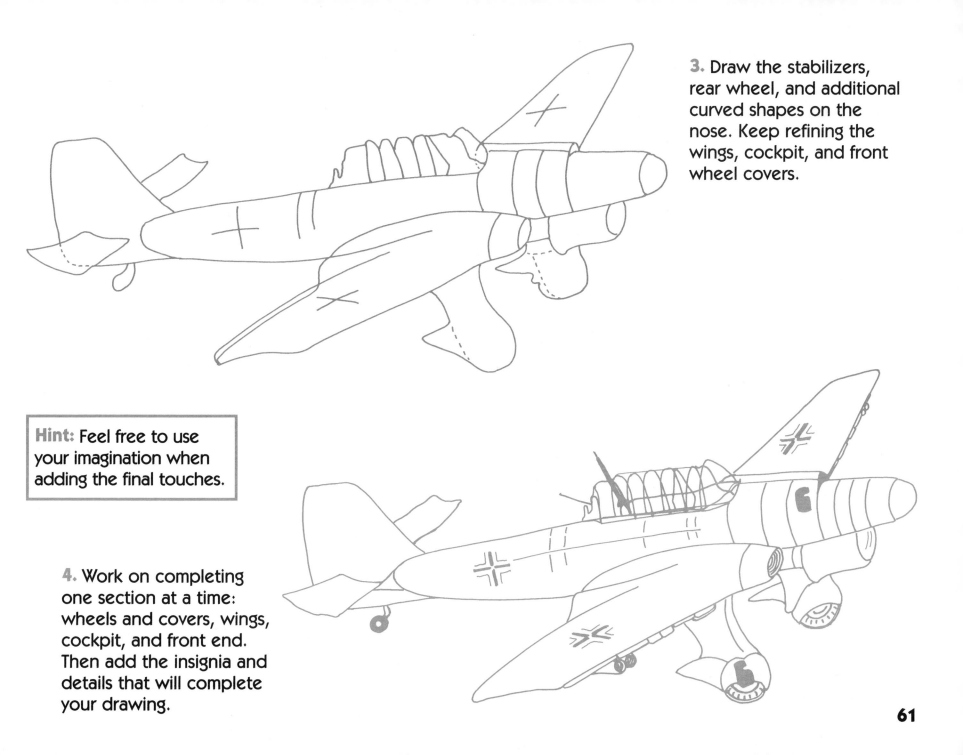

3. Draw the stabilizers, rear wheel, and additional curved shapes on the nose. Keep refining the wings, cockpit, and front wheel covers.

Hint: Feel free to use your imagination when adding the final touches.

4. Work on completing one section at a time: wheels and covers, wings, cockpit, and front end. Then add the insignia and details that will complete your drawing.

61

LCAC (HOVERCRAFT)

The U.S. Navy's LCAC—landing craft, air-cushioned—is a high-speed vessel used to sweep personnel and equipment from ship to shore. It moves over water and land on a "cushion" of air, which takes four gas-turbine engines: two for lift, two for propulsion.

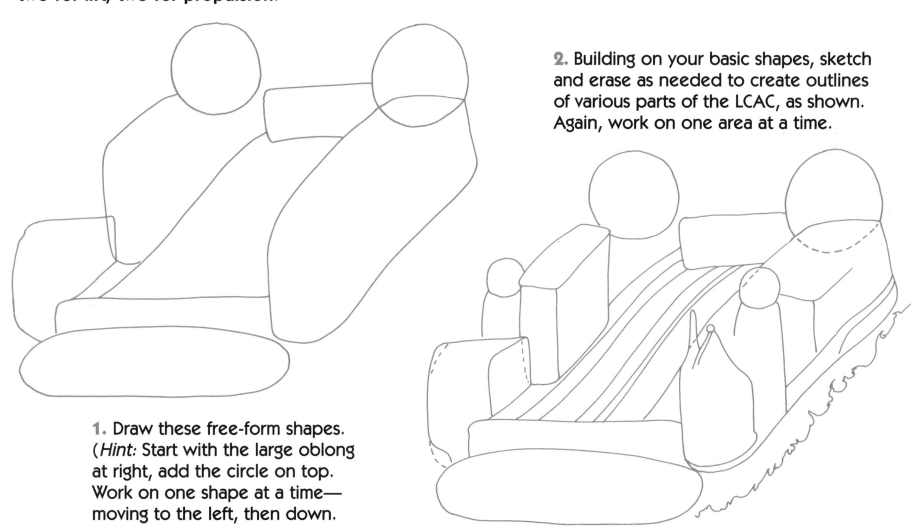

2. Building on your basic shapes, sketch and erase as needed to create outlines of various parts of the LCAC, as shown. Again, work on one area at a time.

1. Draw these free-form shapes. (*Hint:* Start with the large oblong at right, add the circle on top. Work on one shape at a time— moving to the left, then down.

3. Now you can start to fill in more details, such as the propulsion fans and the blocks for the engines and operating equipment. Do not go on to step 4 until you have a clean outline you are satisfied with.

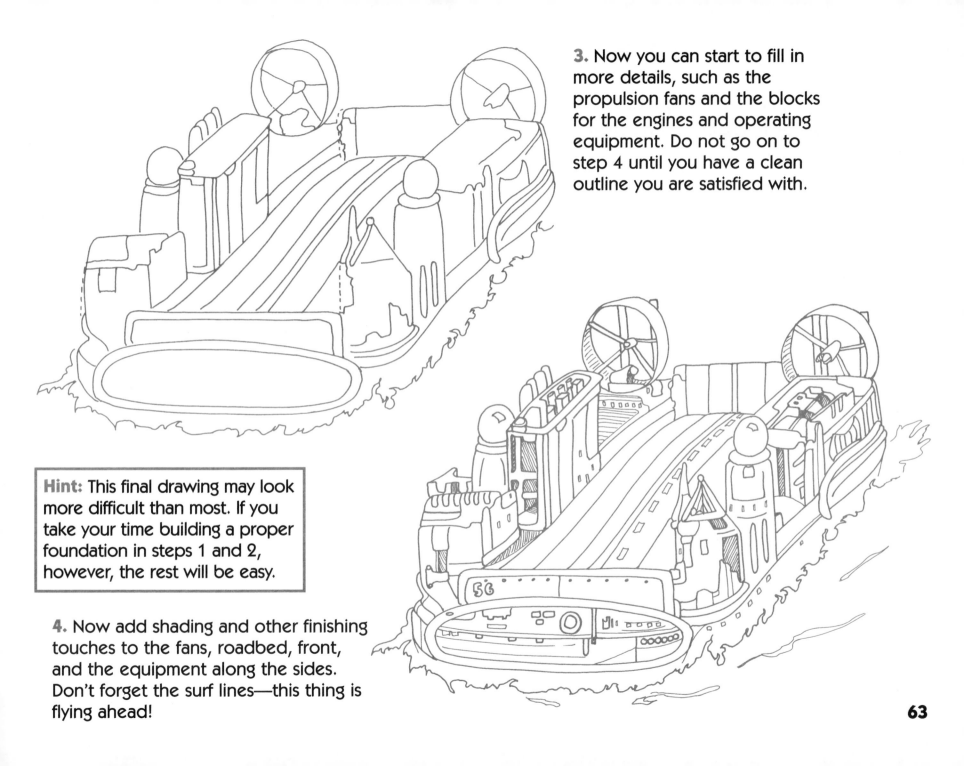

Hint: This final drawing may look more difficult than most. If you take your time building a proper foundation in steps 1 and 2, however, the rest will be easy.

4. Now add shading and other finishing touches to the fans, roadbed, front, and the equipment along the sides. Don't forget the surf lines—this thing is flying ahead!

M109A6 PALADIN

The Paladin is a 155-mm self-propelled howitzer (short cannon) currently in use by U.S. mechanized artillery units.

2. Begin shaping and dividing the basic shapes into sections, adding guidelines for the tire treads. Erase guidelines you no longer need.

1. Draw two rectangular shapes, one atop the other. Then add the carrot-shaped howitzer.

Tip: Notice how foreshortening *(see p. 3)* is used in this drawing, especially for the shape of the long, forward-pointing gun muzzle.

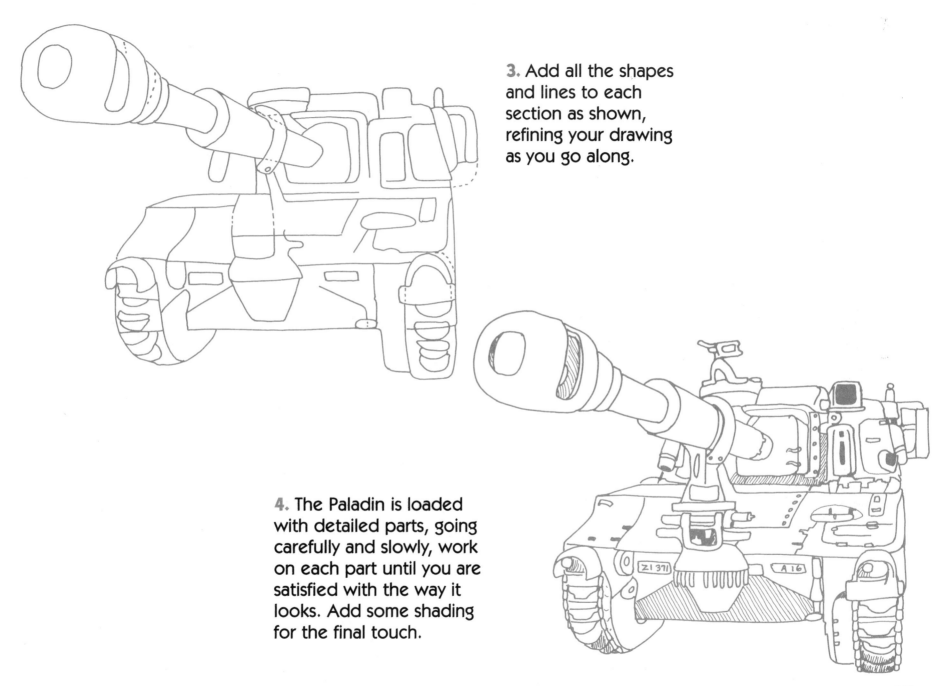

3. Add all the shapes and lines to each section as shown, refining your drawing as you go along.

4. The Paladin is loaded with detailed parts, going carefully and slowly, work on each part until you are satisfied with the way it looks. Add some shading for the final touch.

ZI 371

A 16

BTR-70

This armored, amphibious personnel carrier from Ukraine can float for up to 12 hours. The troop compartment holds six infantry, each equipped with a firing port and vision block.

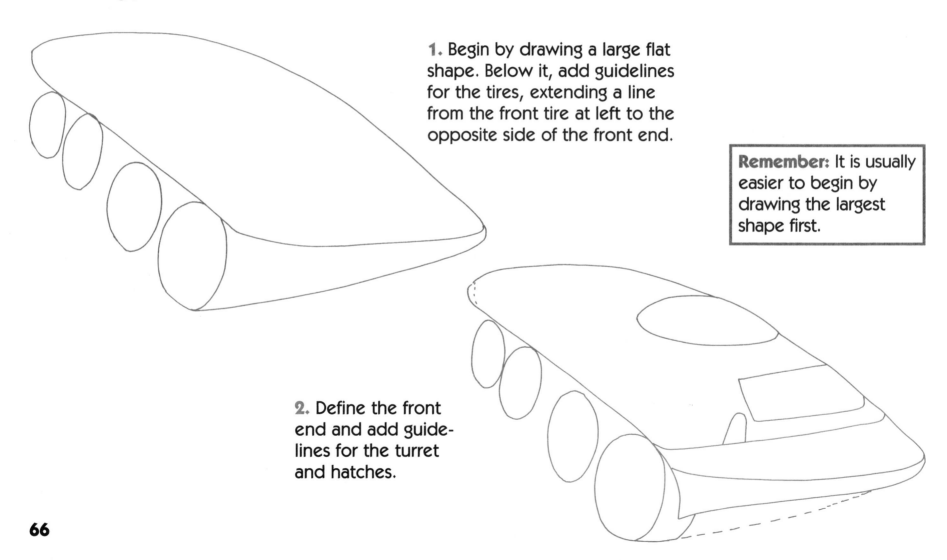

1. Begin by drawing a large flat shape. Below it, add guidelines for the tires, extending a line from the front tire at left to the opposite side of the front end.

Remember: It is usually easier to begin by drawing the largest shape first.

2. Define the front end and add guidelines for the turret and hatches.

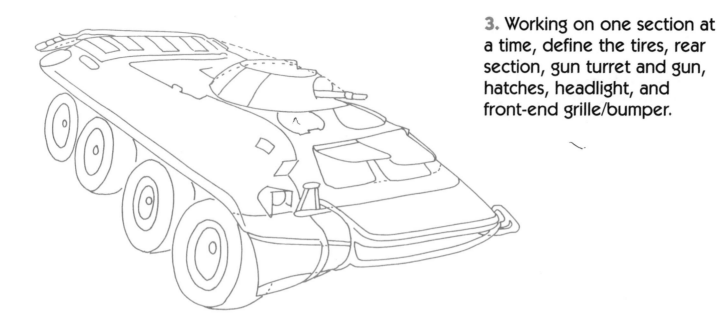

3. Working on one section at a time, define the tires, rear section, gun turret and gun, hatches, headlight, and front-end grille/bumper.

4. Complete, blend, and refine all the lines and shapes together. Add the heavy tire treads and details, and you're ready for anything!

P-38 LIGHTNING

The P-38 Lightning, or "Fork-tailed Devil," could fly farther and at a greater height than any other fighter used in WWII. It carried four .50-caliber machine guns and one 20-millimeter cannon—the only U.S. plane to do so.

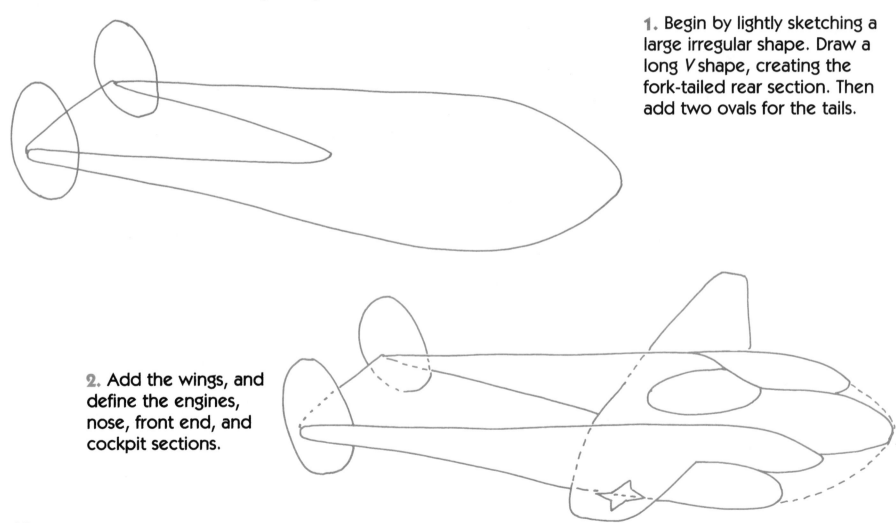

1. Begin by lightly sketching a large irregular shape. Draw a long *V* shape, creating the fork-tailed rear section. Then add two ovals for the tails.

2. Add the wings, and define the engines, nose, front end, and cockpit sections.

3. Complete the stabilizer between the two tails. Add the propellers and refine the cockpit and front end of the P-38. Make sure that you have a smooth, clean outline before adding the final touches.

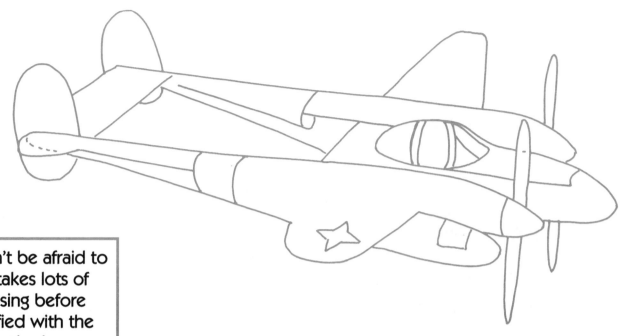

Remember: Don't be afraid to erase. It usually takes lots of drawing and erasing before you will be satisfied with the way your drawing looks.

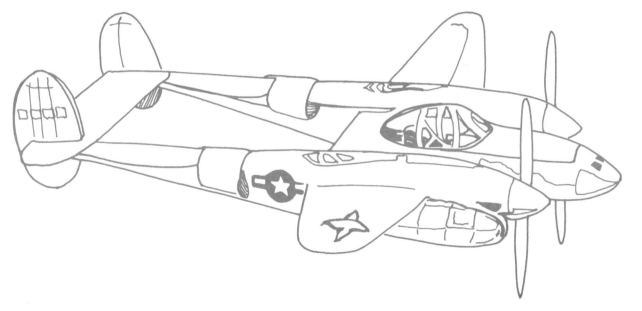

4. Add all the details that made the P-38 a fearsome WWII sky fighter.

U.S.S. LAKE ERIE

The U.S.S. *Lake Erie* is a guided-missile cruiser in the U.S. Navy's test-ship program for theater ballistic missile defense (TBMD).

1. Lightly draw the long horizontal shapes for the hull and deck. Add the basic vertical guideline shapes.

2. Define the tower outlines, erasing unneeded guidelines as you go along. Then start adding the additional lines and shapes.

70

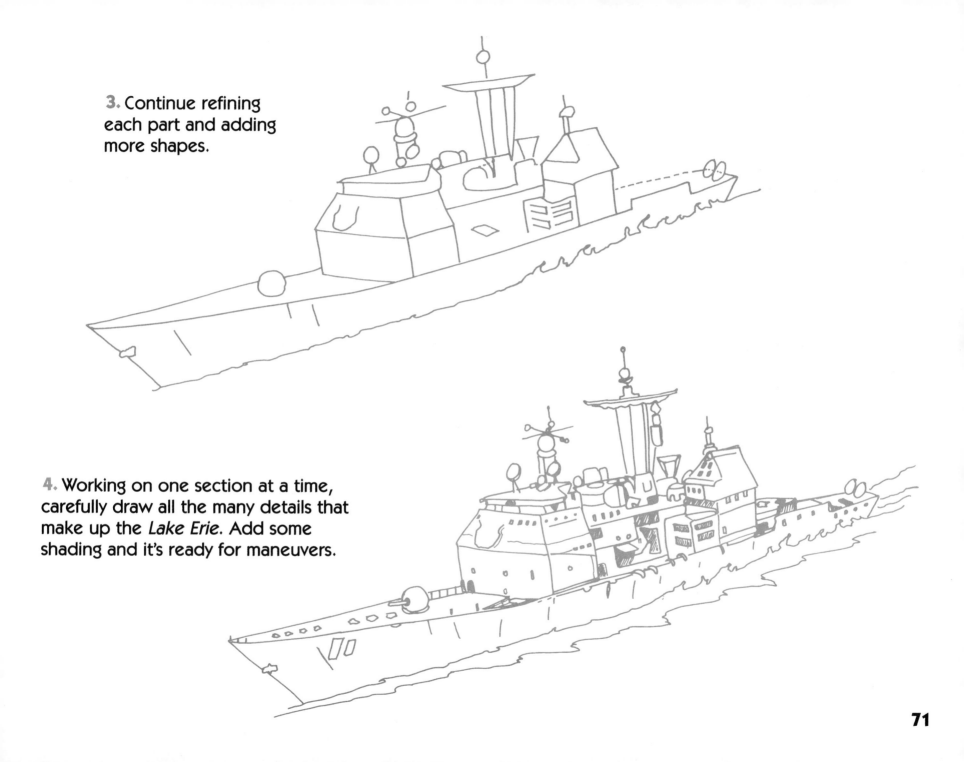

3. Continue refining each part and adding more shapes.

4. Working on one section at a time, carefully draw all the many details that make up the *Lake Erie*. Add some shading and it's ready for maneuvers.

F-117 STEALTH FIGHTER

Also known as the Nighthawk, this plane was the first-ever "stealth" aircraft. Its "skin" absorbs radar waves while its body design scatters the waves, making the aircraft appear as a small bird on radar screens.

Tip: Note that the plane's right wing is drawn short and wide, with the left wing thinner and longer. This technique, called foreshortening *(see p. 3)*, gives the drawing an appearance of depth.

1. Draw a large boomerang-shaped *V.* Complete the fuselage and wings.

2. Add the tails and begin creating the various fuselage sections.

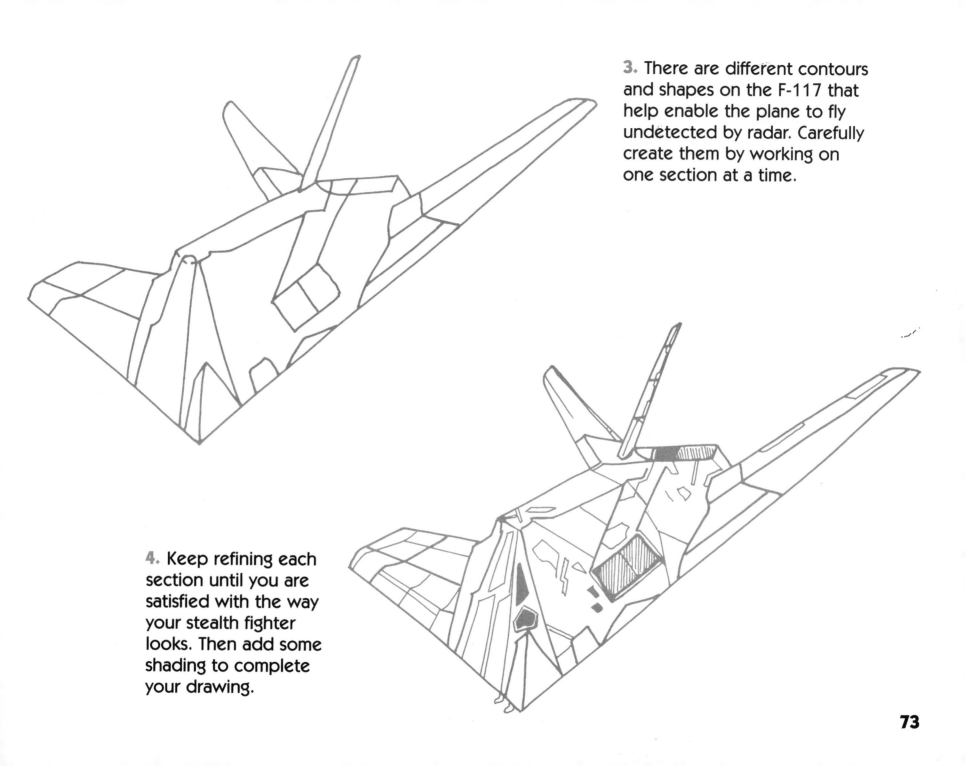

3. There are different contours and shapes on the F-117 that help enable the plane to fly undetected by radar. Carefully create them by working on one section at a time.

4. Keep refining each section until you are satisfied with the way your stealth fighter looks. Then add some shading to complete your drawing.

CHALLENGER

The United Kingdom's heavily-armored MBT (main battle tank) entered service in 1983. The four-person crew controls a 120-mm main gun, two machine guns, and smoke launchers.

1. Draw the basic tank-body outline. Add the basic shapes for the turret and long cannon.

2. Add the hatch on top of the turret, then draw a line along the side of the body, as shown.

74

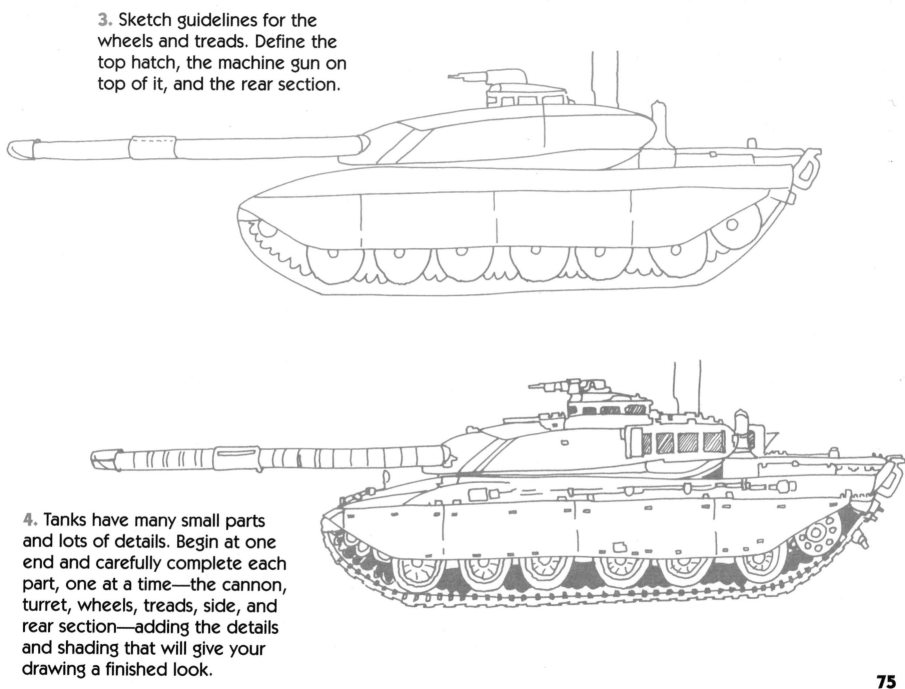

3. Sketch guidelines for the wheels and treads. Define the top hatch, the machine gun on top of it, and the rear section.

4. Tanks have many small parts and lots of details. Begin at one end and carefully complete each part, one at a time—the cannon, turret, wheels, treads, side, and rear section—adding the details and shading that will give your drawing a finished look.

F-4U CORSAIR

One of the great air fighting machines of WWII, the fast, rugged, carrier-borne fighter Corsair packed a great punch with its six machine guns and considerable bomb load.

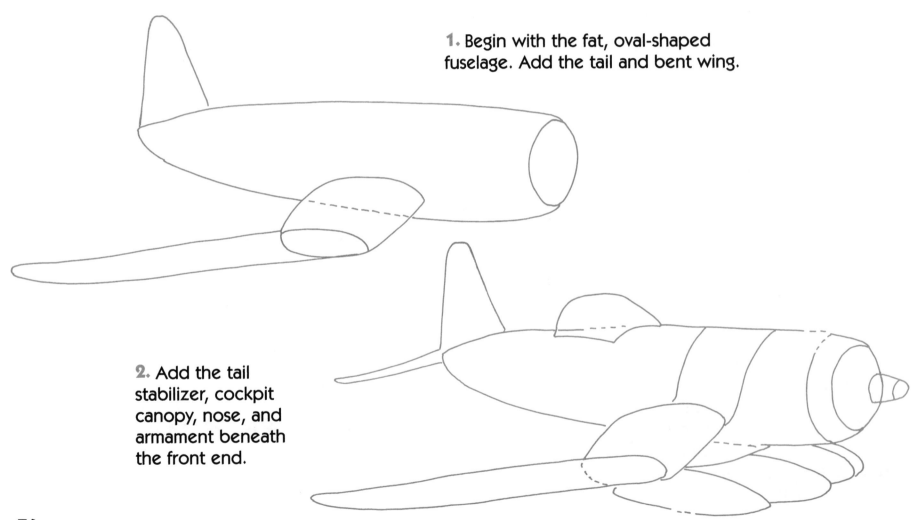

1. Begin with the fat, oval-shaped fuselage. Add the tail and bent wing.

2. Add the tail stabilizer, cockpit canopy, nose, and armament beneath the front end.

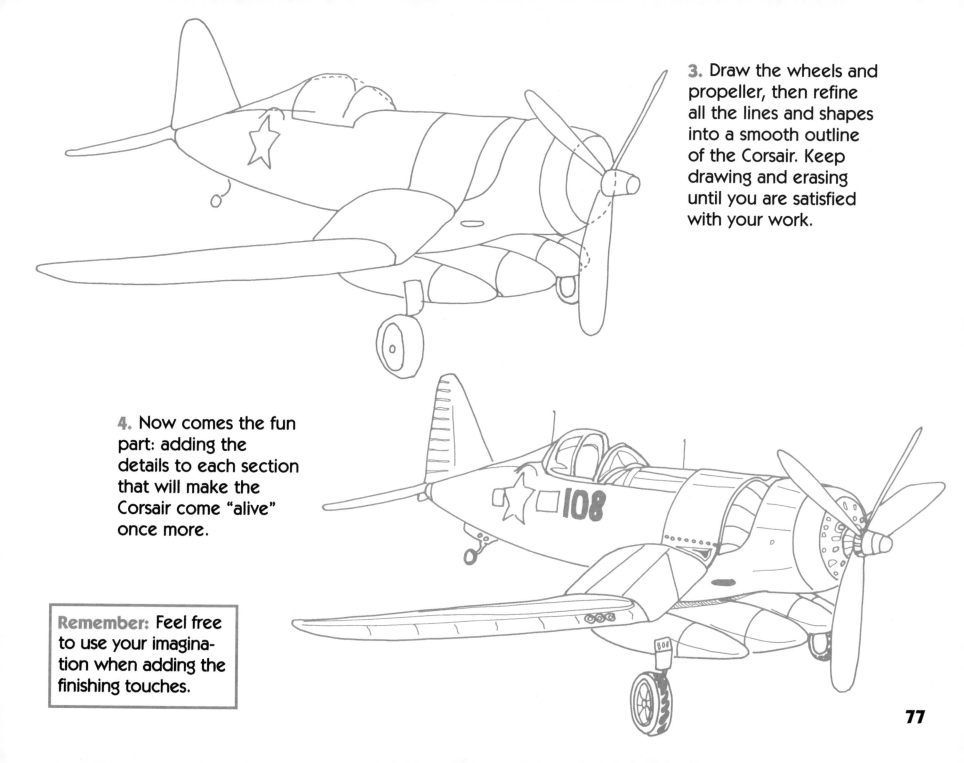

3. Draw the wheels and propeller, then refine all the lines and shapes into a smooth outline of the Corsair. Keep drawing and erasing until you are satisfied with your work.

4. Now comes the fun part: adding the details to each section that will make the Corsair come "alive" once more.

Remember: Feel free to use your imagination when adding the finishing touches.

108

PIRANHA III

The amphibious Piranha III AVGP (armored vehicle, general purpose) has become a favorite choice of military forces throughout the world. It can provide fire support as well as mobility and protection for an 11-person infantry section.

1. Starting with the main body section, lightly sketch the basic shapes as shown.

2. Refine the body, then add the turret and gun on top. Next, create the tires.

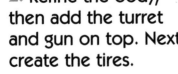

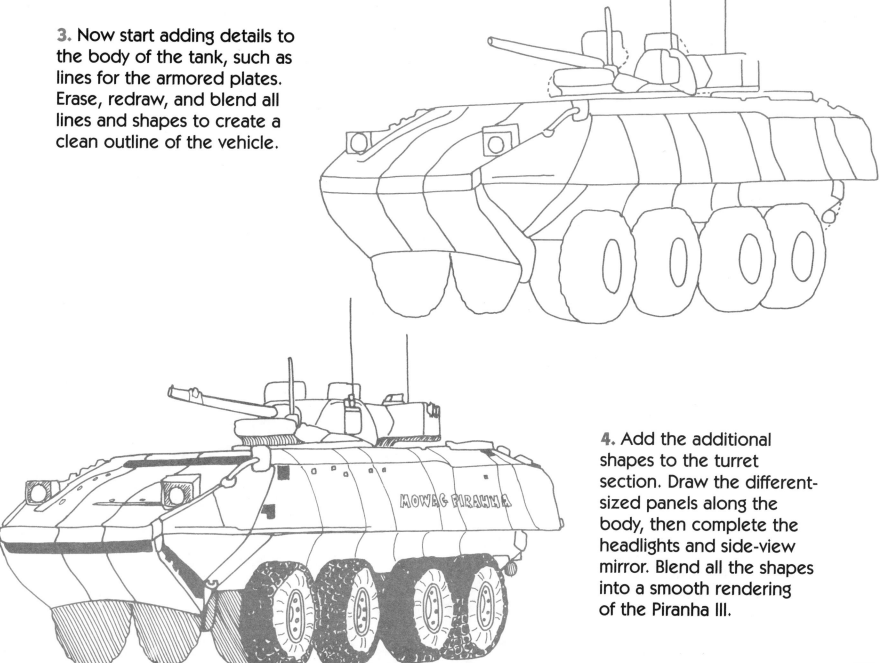

3. Now start adding details to the body of the tank, such as lines for the armored plates. Erase, redraw, and blend all lines and shapes to create a clean outline of the vehicle.

4. Add the additional shapes to the turret section. Draw the different-sized panels along the body, then complete the headlights and side-view mirror. Blend all the shapes into a smooth rendering of the Piranha III.

MOWAG PIRANHA

SPY TANK

A spy tank such as this one—complete with small robots—is on the U.S. Army's list of "dream machines." The Army hopes to deploy these remote-controlled spy tanks someday.

1. To begin, draw an oval on top of a free-form rectangular shape. Put a triangular shape on top of the oval.

2. Add semicircles to the bottom to form wheels, and the basic shapes on top. Sketch the ramp at the front of the tank, then draw an oval on top of it.

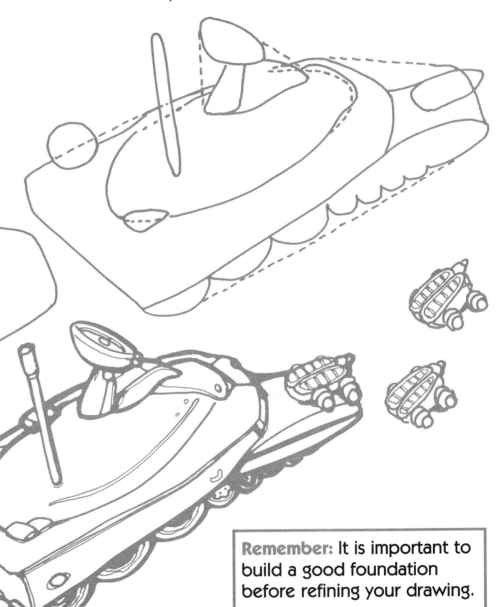

3. Complete the details on the tank, such as a satellite dish and a periscope. Finish the robot on the ramp, then add one or two more on the ground.

Remember: It is important to build a good foundation before refining your drawing.

STEALTH BOMBER

This incredible plane can avoid detection anywhere. The shape (called a "flying wing") and materials used to build the plane absorb and scatter radar signals, therefore making it hard to detect. Its engines are quiet and its exhaust is cooled before it leaves the plane, so that the enemy can't find it.

Remember: It is easy to draw almost anything if you first break it down into simple shapes.

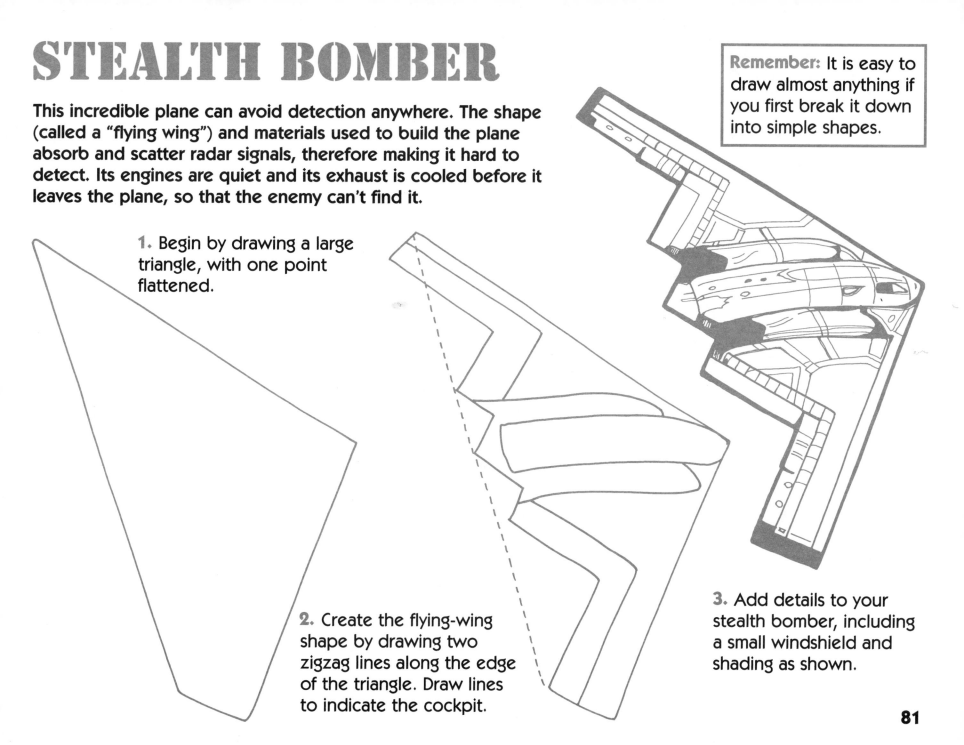

1. Begin by drawing a large triangle, with one point flattened.

2. Create the flying-wing shape by drawing two zigzag lines along the edge of the triangle. Draw lines to indicate the cockpit.

3. Add details to your stealth bomber, including a small windshield and shading as shown.

B-52 STRATOFORTRESS

The B-52 is a long-range heavy bomber capable of flying at high subsonic speeds at altitudes up to 55,000 feet. It can carry a wide array of weapons, including nuclear, gravity, or precision-guided conventional bombs and missiles.

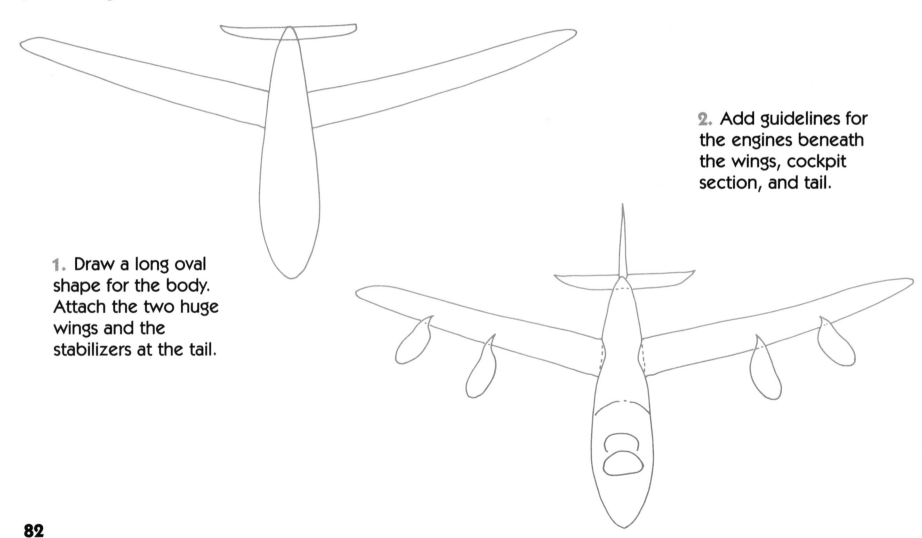

1. Draw a long oval shape for the body. Attach the two huge wings and the stabilizers at the tail.

2. Add guidelines for the engines beneath the wings, cockpit section, and tail.

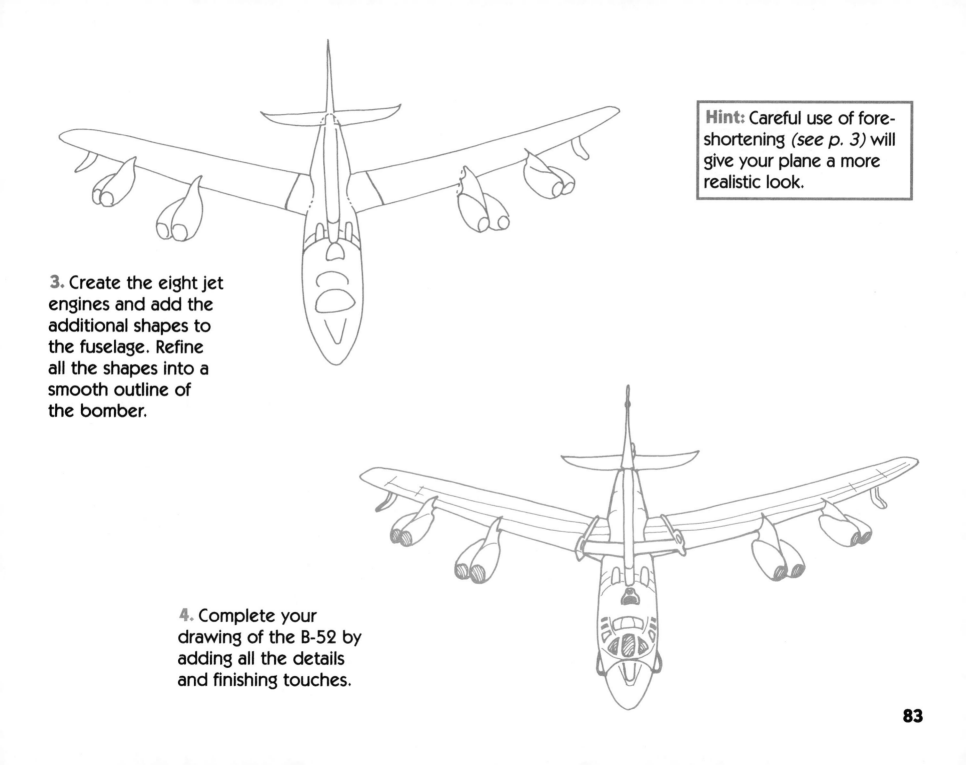

Hint: Careful use of fore-shortening *(see p. 3)* will give your plane a more realistic look.

3. Create the eight jet engines and add the additional shapes to the fuselage. Refine all the shapes into a smooth outline of the bomber.

4. Complete your drawing of the B-52 by adding all the details and finishing touches.

PT BOAT

The PT (patrol torpedo) boat was a small, wooden craft that could sink a battleship or sneak right up to shore to perform reconnaissance or drop off troops. It carried four torpedoes fired from tubes on the side of the boat. During WWII, John F. Kennedy (later the 35th U.S. president) served on a PT boat, PT 109, in the Pacific.

Remember: If, at any time, you don't like the way something looks, erase it and start again.

1. Sketch the large shape for the hull, then sketch the smaller basic shapes on top.

2. Lightly draw guidelines for the sections on the deck. Add some sea foam along the hull of the speedy PT boat.

3. Start defining the torpedo tubes, small guns, and deck stations, erasing any guidelines you no longer need.

4. Complete the torpedo tubes, gun turrets, and all the details that will make this vessel seaworthy again.

F-15E EAGLE

The twin-engine F-15E Eagle is an all-weather, extremely maneuverable tactical fighter designed to gain and maintain air superiority in aerial combat. It can penetrate enemy defenses and out-perform and outfight any current fighter aircraft.

Remember: It is easy to draw almost anything if you first break it down into simple shapes.

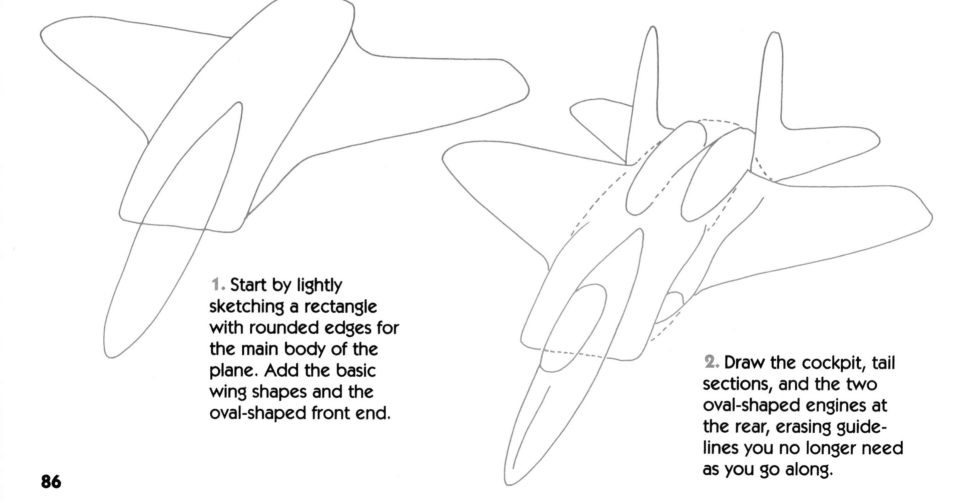

1. Start by lightly sketching a rectangle with rounded edges for the main body of the plane. Add the basic wing shapes and the oval-shaped front end.

2. Draw the cockpit, tail sections, and the two oval-shaped engines at the rear, erasing guide-lines you no longer need as you go along.

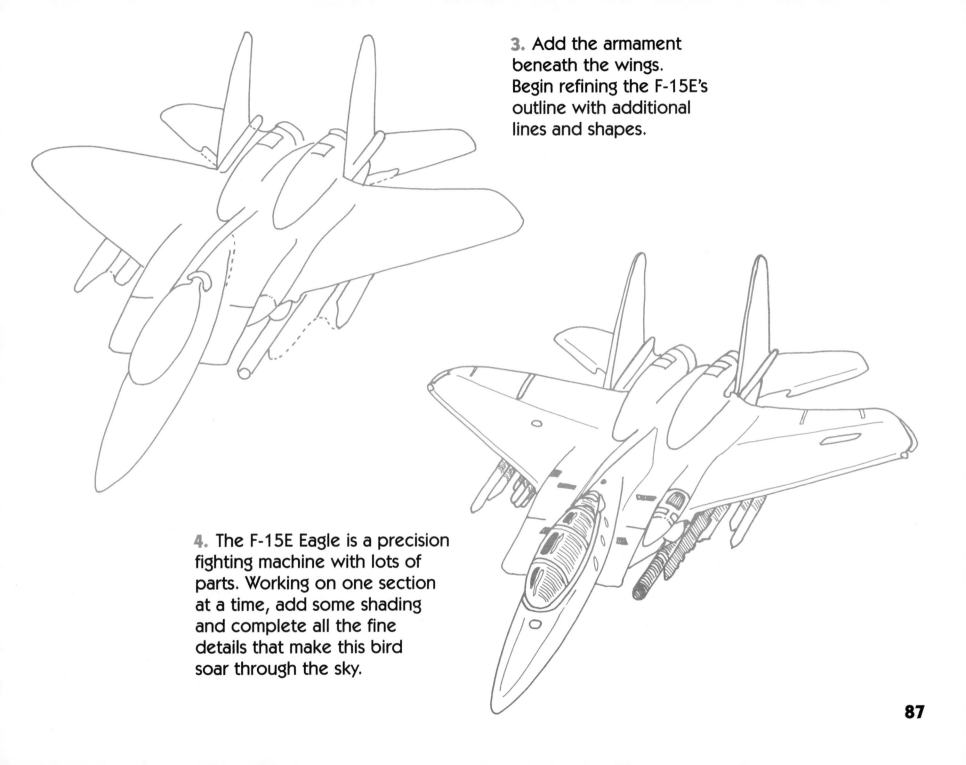

3. Add the armament beneath the wings. Begin refining the F-15E's outline with additional lines and shapes.

4. The F-15E Eagle is a precision fighting machine with lots of parts. Working on one section at a time, add some shading and complete all the fine details that make this bird soar through the sky.

LAV-25

This amphibious personnel carrier, used by the U.S. Army Airborne and the Marine Corps, is air-transportable by helicopter. Several variations exist: air defense, recovery, mortar carrier, command, logistics, and antitank. (*LAV* stands for light armored vehicle.)

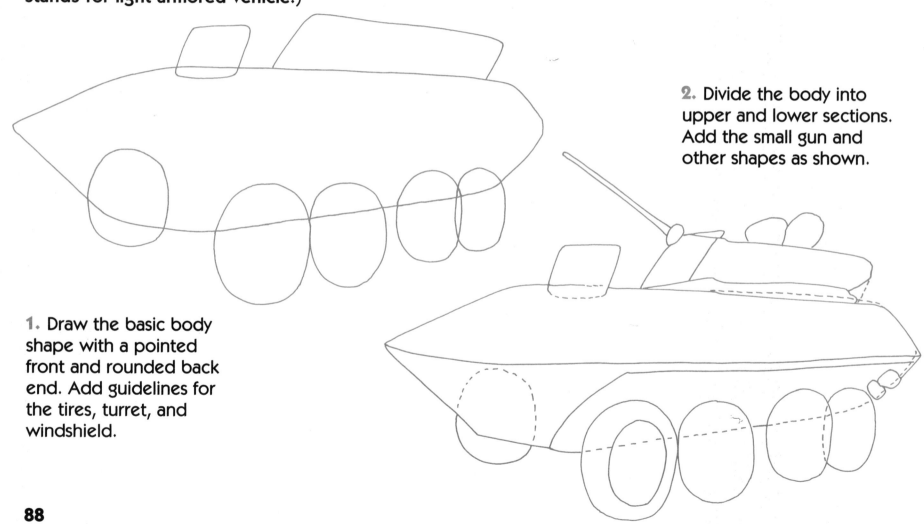

2. Divide the body into upper and lower sections. Add the small gun and other shapes as shown.

1. Draw the basic body shape with a pointed front and rounded back end. Add guidelines for the tires, turret, and windshield.

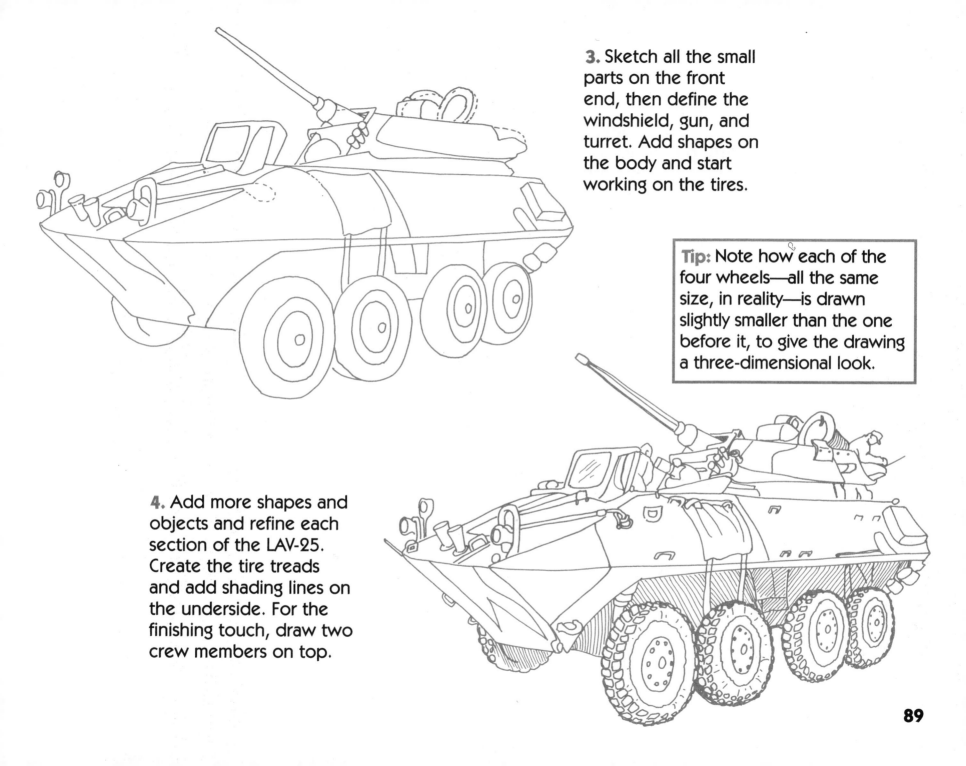

3. Sketch all the small parts on the front end, then define the windshield, gun, and turret. Add shapes on the body and start working on the tires.

Tip: Note how each of the four wheels—all the same size, in reality—is drawn slightly smaller than the one before it, to give the drawing a three-dimensional look.

4. Add more shapes and objects and refine each section of the LAV-25. Create the tire treads and add shading lines on the underside. For the finishing touch, draw two crew members on top.

89

DD-21 ZUMWALT-CLASS DESTROYER

The multimission DD-21 was designed to integrate land, sea, and air attacks and to operate close to hostile shores. Scheduled to be launched in the year 2010, the DD-21 is equipped with precision missiles and guns that can deliver fire 1,000 miles inland.

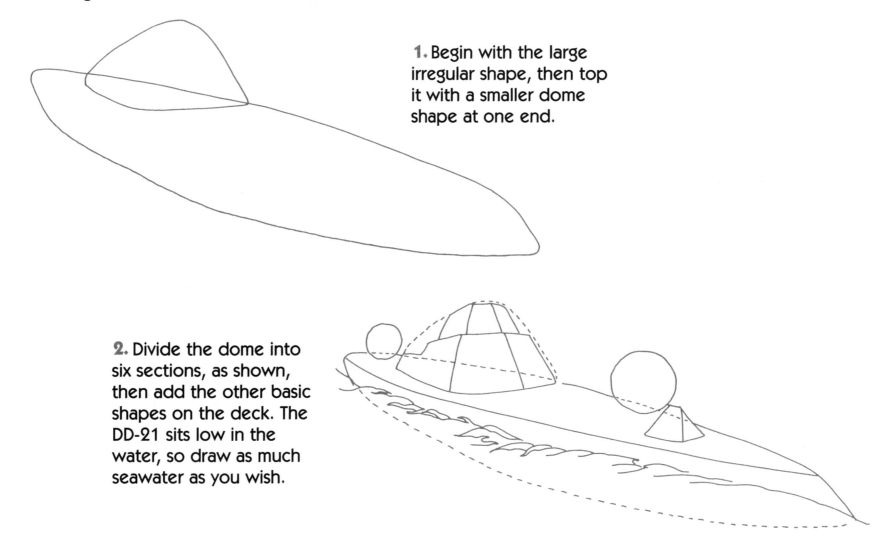

1. Begin with the large irregular shape, then top it with a smaller dome shape at one end.

2. Divide the dome into six sections, as shown, then add the other basic shapes on the deck. The DD-21 sits low in the water, so draw as much seawater as you wish.

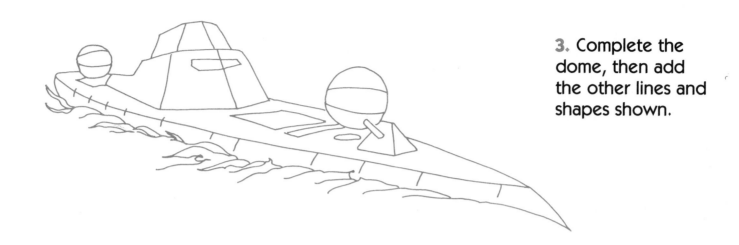

3. Complete the dome, then add the other lines and shapes shown.

Remember: Don't go on to step 4 until you are completely satisfied with the way your drawing looks in step 3.

4. Refine the two spheres and add details. This destroyer has now been launched!

B-17 FLYING FORTRESS

The Flying Fortress—one of the most famous U.S. airplanes ever built—served in every WWII combat zone. It is best remembered for daylight strategic bombing of industrial targets. It had a range of 3,400 miles and could carry 6,000 pounds of bombs.

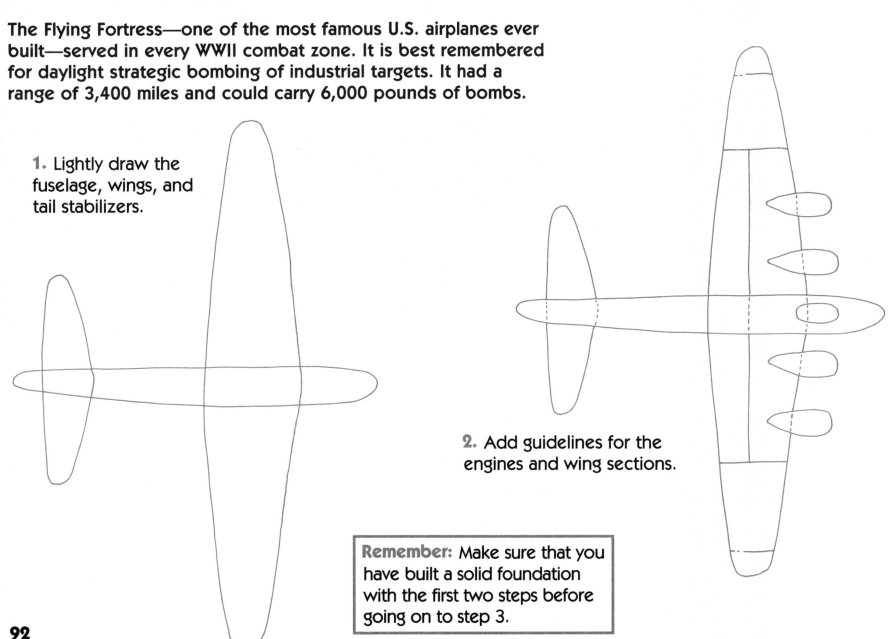

1. Lightly draw the fuselage, wings, and tail stabilizers.

2. Add guidelines for the engines and wing sections.

Remember: Make sure that you have built a solid foundation with the first two steps before going on to step 3.

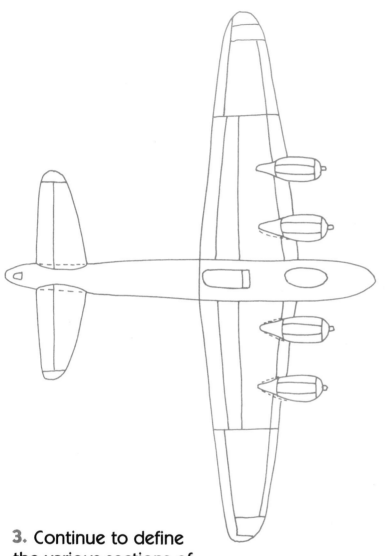

4. Draw each gun turret, from nose to tail, all along the B-17's body. Refine the engines and add all the lines and details on the wings, stabilizers, and fuselage to complete your Flying Fortress.

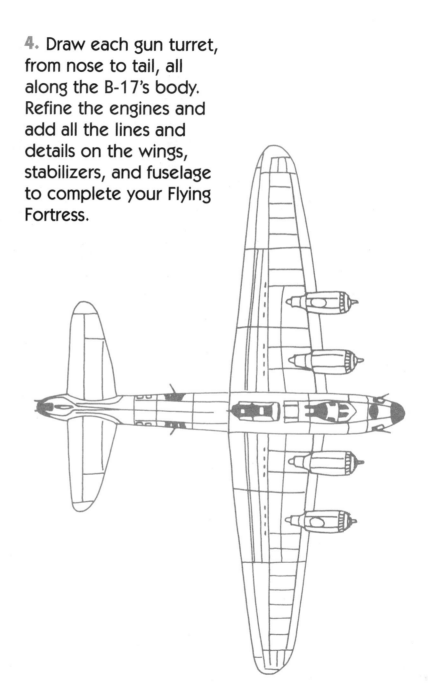

3. Continue to define the various sections of the wings, engines, and tail section. Add the additional shapes as shown.

INDEX

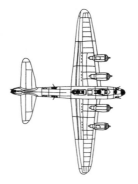

F-15E Eagle
page 86

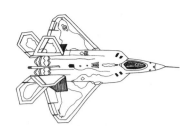

F-22 Raptor
page 12

F-4U Corsair
page 76

F-5E Tiger
turbo jet
page 8

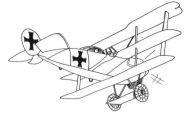

Fokker Dr. I
triplane
page 32

HMMV
(Humvee)
page 50

Junkers
Ju-87 Stuka
page 60

LAV-25
page 88

LCAC
(hovercraft)
page 62

LVTP-7
page 42

M109A6 Paladin
page 64

Minerva
page 30

P-38 Lightning
page 68

Pennington's
invention
page 56

Piranha III
page 78

PT boat
page 84

S-37 Berkut
page 38

Spy tank
page 80

Stealth bomber
page 81

T-80 battle tank
page 36

2S1 SP howitzer
page 58

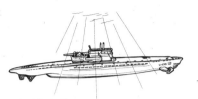

U-boat
page 24

U.S.S. *Arizona*
page 18

U.S.S.
Constitution
page 6

U.S.S. *Essex*
page 10

U.S.S. *Lake Erie*
page 70

U.S.S. *Nautilus*
page 17

World War I tank
page 22

World War II tank
page 4

X-45A UCAV
page 52

XM-8 tank
page 16

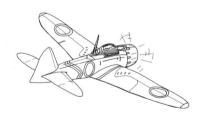

Zero
(A6m Reisen)
page 46